I0162696

From *Giovanni* to *Johnny*

One boy, two cultures, some setbacks, but living happily ever laughter.

Johnny-Giovanni Piazza

ISBN-10: 0692594957
ISBN-13: 9780692594957

ACKNOWLEDGMENTS
Pat Piazza Falting
Rosario Piazza
John Selloriquez

I would also like to express my gratitude to all of those doubters. If not for your mockery, this book would never have been written. *Johnny-Giovanni Piazza*

Preface

Somehow, I lived two lives simultaneously, old-country tradition at home and the American life I strived for when away. I had two names, Giovanni and Johnny. I couldn't escape from reality and what I had wished for seldom came true. My experiences and genetic design destined me to be who I am today. Writing about the "oops" and "ahhs" of life helped release an aberrant presence housed in my soul for years that made me sometimes question my own relevance. "Your evil time is up, out I say, and never return!"

The beginning was decades ago with Italian immigrant grandparents, a tough, old-school father and a loving mother. At times, I questioned my parents, our nation, its people, and my friends. I blamed some of my failures on being Italian rather than blaming myself. The truth being, sometimes I was just not good enough. I can be found in the Auld Lang Syne section of my lost loves and can only wonder what might have been.

Throughout my life, I was staggered with some destructive doses of reality that I didn't see coming, but I survived. Time, places, events, and people have refined me to a smiling trace of evidence that God does exist and He cares.

I was Giovanni and I am Johnny.

A Tribute to My Italian Family

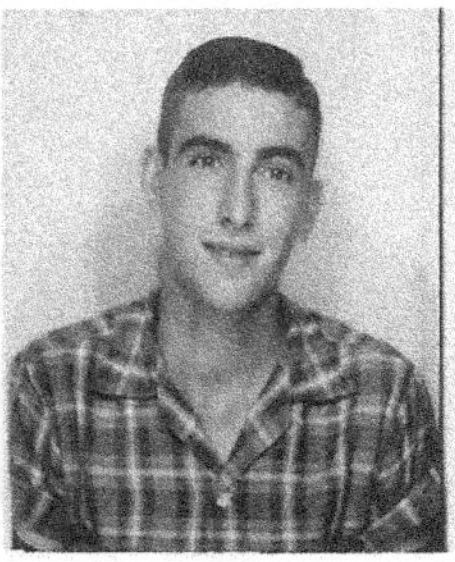

Welcome to America!

Smile, say Mozzarella Cheese!

Contents

Part One Being Giovanni

Part Two School Days and Nights

Part Three The Sixties Scene

Part Four Football, Friends, and a Broken Heart

been. Nevertheless, the most difficult thing about being myself is that I always feel like I'm losing.

I humbly express my gratitude to those who have been part of my life's unusual story. I love each of you as you are and would like your forgiveness for the times I failed you. Our time together was not long enough. That is what makes it so special! Thanks for sharing some of your life with me. I hope you enjoy the book and like me, live happily ever laughter! *Vi amo tutti.*

Warning: This book is rated R for Real. The following pages contain stories, sarcasm and cynicism you may not be able to believe, handle, understand or like. I don't apologize.

Part One Being Giovanni

Chapter 1

I Was Made in America

September 9th I was born
Smelled the roses, felt the thorns
Mom and Dad were sometimes sad
But in the end I hope they were glad
Johnny-Giovanni

I was born a second generation Italian, strike one, and a few days later was baptized into the Roman Catholic Church, strike two. My family was sociologically classified as upper lower class, with the emphasis on lower and not upper. However, by God's grace, I was unaware of the classification at that time. Still today, though classifications are meaningless to me, to some they are rules to live by. Most of those minds will never be changed so we "lowers" must find techniques to deal with them.

I thought I was going to be loved, nurtured, and accepted; unfortunately, some people had a different rule book. I made the mistakes of thinking everyone was the same and parents were always loving and supportive. To me, there were no sociological or economic classes. I was an idealist; therefore, a slow learner to reality.

I repeated my mistakes many times over before I said, "Oh yeah, now I know." Even today, I am not educated enough to understand the lack of kindness, compassion, or mercy by some when it comes to accepting other human beings. I lived a lot of my youth and some of my adult life trying not to feel inferior to others even though most of my friends, co-workers, neighbors, teammates, and strangers have been very respectful. The challenge is, how do we respond when they are not?

During the period from 1900-1910, a large number of immigrants came to the United States. The vast majority of Italians were from southern Italy. My grandparents were from the coastal city Cefalu on the

Italian island of Sicily. They were referred to as Sicilians. Once in America, they congregated together in small communities and spoke their native language. This lifestyle offered a sense of security. Their neighborhoods were often called "Little Italies." Many of the unskilled Italians entered the food business beginning as fruit and vegetable vendors. They graduated from wagons, to trucks, to small grocery stores, and then to restaurants.

Bilingual homes prevailed and I hated it. I would tell my mother not to speak Italian if my friends were coming over. I wouldn't have friends over if my father was home; it was too much of a risk. Located on my street was the Italian Moderno, now known as the Progressive Men's Club. Italian wedding receptions, dances, and meetings were held there. It was also a favorite place for politicians seeking the Italian vote.

Over the bridge and across the river
To my grandparents' house we would go
They were Italian and I was an American
This they didn't know
Johnny-Giovanni

My mother and father were first generation Italian-Americans of immigrant parents. My grandparents brought with them their stories and ways of life from the old country. I never understood what they said, because they didn't *speaka da English*. I listened intently, grinning and laughing when cued by their gestures, trying to be respectful. I would mimic their expressions so they were very proud of their little Italian grandson.

As I remember, they would give me a hug and sometimes a sloppy, smelly kiss and proudly say "*Giovanni, Giovanni*!" Why would they always say it twice? After a while, I figured out that was my name, Johnny, in Italian. I guess they couldn't, or didn't prefer to speak English. When were they going to say, *"Arrivederci Roma"* and become true Americans? They never did. I was embarrassed that my grandparents could not speak English. I could not understand them or talk about them to my friends. I was a kid living in two cultures, one fading and one emerging. I do have some regrets today.

My paternal grandfather grew homegrown fruits and vegetables and sold them from the family vehicle, a mule-drawn flatbed wagon. When visiting all day every Sunday, I would sometimes coax a ride from my grandfather on his animal-drawn carriage. As the automobiles passed by, I was thinking how envious people must be of me.

One day I was playing cowboys and Indians with my cousin Peter. He and his mother lived with my grandparents. Peter came out of the house with two guns strapped to his side, a cowboy hat, and a bandana. He jumped into the seat of the wagon while the mule was grazing. I always wanted to be the Indian because I have an affection for the underdog role.

My friend had loaned me his brother's fiberglass bow and I made some arrows from sticks. Peter's toy guns were no match for my fiberglass bow. To be authentic, I took off my shirt and smeared some mud on my chest. I left my jeans on for obvious reasons. I had never seen an Indian on the warpath wearing soiled Jockey shorts. I jumped off the back porch and yelled "Surprise attack!" I launched one of my home-made arrows too far to the left, but with its imperfections it began to break back to the right, skimming the side of Pete's face right past his left eye. I had underestimated the power of the bow.

The arrow drew blood, and Pete began to scream. Immediately, charging out the back door was his mother holding a broom, followed by my grandmother with a large wooden spoon. They were berating me in Italian and chasing me around the yard, but they were no match for my youth and agility. Then I heard the chilling words that stopped me in my tracks: "*I'm agonna tella your father*." I was no longer the brave Indian that shot the arrow. I was reduced to a quivering eight year-old crying, blowing snot bubbles, and begging forgiveness while standing in a puddle of pee.

I was confused about my family while I was growing up. I knew their love and dedication was like no other, but it was too embarrassing to explain to my "American" friends at school. It would only escalate their mocking of my Italian life and my Catholic religion. My family's friends were all Italian. Mine were not. Thus, on one hand I had to totally live the Old Italian life style but also had to keep it a secret and live the lifestyle of my friends to keep their ridicule at a minimum.

I quit wearing my St. Jude medal. I could never explain a St. Joseph altar, me sitting with Jesus at the Last Supper, my grandfather cooking on an open fire in the backyard with a large washtub full of boiling water and spaghetti, or a grape vine trellis on the side of the house. I knew no one would understand a wooden barrel of homemade wine, the old mule tied near the vegetable wagon he would pull the next day through the neighborhood streets, or my grandfather dressed in knickers, suspenders, and knee-high boots patrolling the field of Italian squash. These are not the things you share at show and tell at school. I didn't openly embrace the Italian culture. I couldn't even speak Italian except for the curse words I heard so often. This Giovanni was born in the United States, made in America!

1. Where was the immigration processing center for Europeans in New York?
   A) Staten Island
   B) Ellis Island
   C) Liberty Island

Chapter 2
The Oddfather

My father was one of nine children living in a small house with parents who were new to America. He had two responses for every request I made. The answer was always "No," or for what he deemed a really ridiculous request, "Hell No!"

My father passed away in 1978, but it was just recently that I analyzed why he chose his words so carefully:

1) He was one of nine children of poor immigrant parents.
2) He didn't complete high school.
3) He grew up during the Great Depression of the 1930's.
4) He was drafted into the U.S. Army during World War II.
5) He fought against Germany and Italy, his parents' home country.

Those events probably left psychological issues that could not heal.

I didn't know my dad had fought in WWII until I was about eight years old. He never mentioned it, and neither did anyone else in the family. One day my mom had opened an old trunk that was under lock and key to put away some blankets for the summer. I saw some military medals, two bayonets, a Nazi flag, a stack of German marks, military pictures, scarves, and a Purple Heart. I always thought there was a body in the trunk, because I was told to stay away from it.

When my mother unlocked the trunk, I looked in and shouted, "What are these?" My mother calmly stated, "Those are some things your daddy brought back from the war." I began to rattle off a series of questions before my mother could answer.

"What war?"

"Did he win?"

"How many people did he kill?"

"Is he going to hurt me?" If you had lived with him, you would know those were legitimate questions.

That is one of the many reasons I am so proud of him. He was in combat in a terrible conflict near his parent's homeland, fighting for his adopted country, and yet didn't complain or boast about it. In fact, he never mentioned it. My mother later told me the Purple Heart medal was from shrapnel wounds in his side. It was not known if he would survive. Fortunately for him, he survived. Sometimes, it was not so fortunate for me, but I also survived.

Nevertheless, his parenting skills would be classified Old Mafia. He was totally intimidating, mostly non-verbal, and very physical. When he was verbal, he said words that I knew should not be repeated, yet I was smart enough to know that he didn't mean them. He was the head of the family for sure, the Patriarch. Maybe not the Godfather, but more like the Oddfather.

He didn't raise his voice, but he often raised his fist. Was it tough love or felony assault? Why, of course it was tough love, sometimes too tough. Sometimes there was a case for felony assault. The Oddfather helped me acquire my quick reactions and a body that could absorb pain and punishment anywhere. I learned how to stop, drop and roll when there wasn't a fire.

There was an old classic-Italian song from 1954, *Oh My Papa.* It mentions the words gentle, loveable, good, understanding and wonderful. My dad really was wonderful and good, both as a man and as a father; yet he certainly came up short on being gentle, lovable, and understanding.

I will never forget precursor statements such as "I'll tattoo you" (leave a bruise), or "I'll crown you" (a slap to the top of the head). The closing comment was always, "That's good for you," and everyone would shake their heads, "yes." They knew not to disagree, or they would be the next victim.

The wheels on the car go round and round
The fists in the car go pound and pound
Johnny-Giovanni

My dad bought our first car, a 1948 Dodge, in 1953. It should have been nicknamed the "Death Ride" for the punishment that was inflicted in the small confines between those four doors. Of course, the color was black. Often, I imagined Vincent Price being the chauffeur driving me to the dungeon.

My astute brother would always get in the car first, in the back seat passenger side, behind my mother. He wisely knew that was the safe zone because our father's arms could not reach there from his driver's seat perch. That left the back seat driver side behind my father for me. Since I was an easy target for the backhand over the seat, I tried to find a position as far away from the front as possible. There were two choices: Move towards the middle of the back seat, hoping he couldn't reach me, or tuck myself in the corner behind him, cover up in the fetal position, and make myself as small a target as possible.

I chose the latter. I developed the ability to absorb punishment while riding with him. Sometimes it was a standoff. He could look backward, drive forward, and dodge cars, while I looked forward, shrank backward, and dodged punches. You know what they say, "like father, like son." Appropriately, this all took place in a vehicle called a Dodge. If he would have connected with a few more punches it could not have been called a Dodge. The Dodge Motor Company could have had a new model, the Dodge Homicide.

Once, I made a huge mistake; I spoke while he was driving. Slight movements were allowed, but no talking. Nostradamus-like, I predicted the future, and it was not going to be pleasant. As I glanced into the rear view mirror from the back seat, I saw the eyes of danger. I could hear the hoof beats of the Four Horsemen of the Apocalypse. I could feel their breath on my neck. I didn't have time to "get outta Dodge."

A huge right hand whizzed across the back seat and like a young Muhammad Ali, I moved out of the way by a mere fraction of an inch. This was my introduction to defensive driving: while dad was driving, I was being defensive in the back seat. My movements only made him angrier. He drove the car to the side of the road, stopped and inflicted some "discipline."

Once, I had a birdhouse. I placed it in the backyard atop a post. A blackbird nested there, and the miracle of life happened. I had a whole family of blackbirds, and as a youngster, I felt like a parent. I was the guardian of the blackbird family. As the family grew, however, so did the noise.

My dad was a police officer, working the night shift from 11 P.M. to 7A.M., so it was imperative that we be quiet or away when he was sleeping during the day. I got the memo, but the baby blackbirds didn't.

One day in a rage, he got out of bed and took me outside to the blackbirds' home. He issued an edict of execution for the unknowing birds. Emotions filled my body, but I knew not to show any feelings or I might be joining the birds as a memory.

Sad to the core, I removed my feathery family from the birdhouse and witnessed their execution. Then, I disposed of their bodies. At that moment, I wished I had been one of those blackbirds. You won't find this bird story on an episode of *The Andy Griffith Show.*

My older brother was sometimes responsible for the iron hand of discipline on me. As youngsters, we slept in the same small bed. At bedtime, there was usually laughing, pushing, and fighting for prime sleeping real estate. My dad would appear at the door and say, "Go to sleep. I don't want to hear another peep out of you." As soon as he walked off, my brother would say, "Peep, peep."

The room was dark and when my father would return with uncontrollable anger and a belt, the room became even darker. I don't how it was possible. His presence could make any form of danger worse.

The problem was I always had the side of the bed nearest the doorway, thanks to my brother's strategy. As the belt swung across the darkened room, all I could do was curl up in the fetal position and take the punishment. His swings were accurate even in the dark. Delivered either from the left side or from the right, they were all on target. Sometimes, you just have to stand on the tracks and face the train.

As things quieted down and dad's anger subsided, he would leave the room exhausted from swinging the belt. In baseball jargon, he could hit from both sides of the plate or in boxing, he could really "sling the leather." As he would leave the room, he would repeat, "I don't want to hear another peep out of you." Then, my brother would say, "Peep. Peep," and a new assault began.

I don't regret or blame my father for the heavy-handed discipline (no pun intended) he dealt. He ruled with an iron fist, or at the least, it felt like an iron fist (pun intended). Our experiences make us who we are. He was expecting the American Dream and had to live through the American nightmare of early immigration, poverty, the Great Depression, World War II, and probably some forms of ethnic injustice and me. We were raised as he and many Italians were raised in that era. He was who he was. His experiences and decisions defined him. All is forgiven.

The ultimate form of discipline and humiliation occurred frequently at my grandparent's home. All nine of the siblings would arrive with their families every Sunday after church. The men would sit around trading stories in Italian inserted with some broken English. The women would be preparing the Italian dinner with my grandmother, and the children would be playing among their cousins. Playing would often turn into arguing or fighting.

When I was called into the house for tormenting my cousins, I was greeted with an introductory slap to the back of the head, a hand grabbing one wrist, and another hand landing blows to my butt. I would unknowingly be doing the Mambo Italiano dance of humiliation while swats from Dad's hand rained down on the moving target, my ass.

I tried my best to block the blows with my free hand. I ran in circles to lessen the force of the blows. The impact of his hand on my butt was creating forward momentum on my six-year-old body. That's how I acquired my speed at an early age. I was a victim of hit and run. The more he hit, the faster I would run. I often wondered how many more laps I had to run around him to get to the finish line.

The men, women, and cousins always laughed at the punishment as entertainment. My butt was sore, and my legs were tired. The taunting would continue outside with a sarcastic, "You gotta whippin'! You gotta whippin'!" My face-saving reply was, "Yea, but I didn't cry."

However, if I had cried, the thrashing would have continued and Dad would yell, “Stop crying like a baby” until the tears ceased. To cry or not to cry, that was the question. I learned not to cry.

Italian fathers loved their boys but didn’t want them to show emotion. It was considered a sign of weakness. Italian mothers really loved their boys but knew not to intervene in the discipline of a son. They could become the recipient of the same punishment they were trying to prevent.

I was proud of my parents, and I know they were proud of me because I could whip the ass of any of my cousins, if necessary. In fact, I held the top spot on the pyramid of cousins. I had my father to thank for that. Like the famous Italian football coach Vince Lombardi said, “Winning isn’t everything; it’s the only thing.”

There is a special bond between Italian mothers and her sons. They provide the voice of reason and emotional security that Italian fathers ignore. My mother did not have an easy life, but she made life easy for me. She was faithful to the family throughout the darkest times, some so dark that I never want to think about them and surely won’t write about them. “Honor thy father and thy mother.”

I do not have one negative recollection of my mother. When my father would answer, “Hell, No!” she would find a hidden way to make it a silent “Hell, Yes!” Whenever I wanted sports equipment, toys, money to go out, a gift for a girlfriend, or to go to some places I probably shouldn’t be, she always found a way to give me the money or the confidence that I needed. Whatever cover-up or sacrifice she had to make, she always did it. She took me to practice, picked me up after practice, and attended all my games; the exact opposite of my father.

My mother was also the religious leader of the home. She instilled the Catholic values in our lives and lived them until her death. Ironically, she died on Good Friday, 1980. We walked to mass every Sunday, every holy day of obligation, and for any church function. If I was not paying attention in church, she would pinch me on the thigh or beneath the armpit, but that was as violent as she ever got. Her love mended my pain many times. She is still protecting me decades after her death.

Chapter 3
Little Italy

My first home was in the Italian section of Shreveport, Louisiana. It was a rented, three-bedroom, wooden house on cinder blocks. My favorite entertainment in the summer was the minor league class Double A baseball team the “Sports.” Texas League Park was only one block from my house on the corner of Sycamore Avenue and Dove Street and across the street from the elementary school I attended.

From school, I could look from the playground and see the covered bleachers and the tower of lights of this sports temple. My mother, my brother, and I would walk to the stadium and root, root, root for the home team. I remember those cream-colored home uniforms with “SPORTS” in red, trimmed in navy blue arched across the chest. Those players, my heroes, wore navy blue baseball caps with a red bill and a white letter “S.” They won the Texas League Playoffs in 1952 and 1955 and won the Texas League Pennant in 1954. In my mind, I can still hear the public address announcer calling out the lineup.

“At third base, Jim Ackerett.”

“At shortstop, Joe Koppe.”

“Second baseman, Chico Garcia.”

“At first base, John Jones.”

“And behind the plate, J.W. Jones.”

I yearned for the day when my name would be called over the speakers and everyone would cheer.

When the game was over, I would rush to the railing and ask for a baseball or a cracked bat. In 1956, Ken Guettler, an outfielder for the Sports, hit sixty-two home runs. To me, it was the greatest accomplishment of all mankind. When I went home, I pretended to be Ken Guettler while hitting rocks with my broomstick bat. I would trot around the yard after a home run and listen to the crowd cheer for the rock that I had just launched across the street.

When it was time for my team to be on the field, I would put on my glove and throw a rubber ball against the house and catch or chase the ricocheting ball to all parts of the yard. Once, I got one of my white tee shirts and took a red crayon and wrote "SPORTS" across the chest. It was my first baseball uniform.

When playing in the house
And committing a blunder
Run as fast as you can
Safety lies down under
Johnny-Giovanni

Our front porch extended the width of the house. It provided a great place to play on rainy days. The cinder blocks allowed me to hide under the house whenever I was in trouble from things such as a broken window, stealing money, or one of my bigger blunders.

One of my early ambitions was to be a paper boy. A paper boy had to throw papers toward a house, so accuracy was imperative. One day, I was practicing in the house. I folded some old newspapers and began throwing them toward the corners of the walls, under tables, or between furniture. As my confidence grew, I recklessly threw one that wiped out everything on the fireplace mantle, including Grandma's and Grandpa's picture, a vase, a small lamp that was now rendered broken beyond repair, and poor, old St. Jude's statue. All the king's horses and all the king's men couldn't put St. Jude together again.

Before the crash was complete, I was out the door and to the safe haven under the house. I did a lot of thinking, crying, and praying while there in my make-shift chapel, which was too small for an adult.

I promised to give up my paper delivery ambitions if my parents would allow me to return inside and not discipline me. I kept my part of the agreement; they didn't.

2. What is the original definition of a ghetto?
   A) A poor neighborhood
   B) An ethnic neighborhood
   C) A crime ridden neighborhood

Remember in the movie *Porky's,* when the boys had a penis contest? The Italian boys in my neighborhood had a nose contest to see who had the largest nose. The contest was won by Nicky Stephano, who forever became "Nicky the Nose." Having any nickname was reputable in "Little Italy." What love we had for each other!

There were small Italian businesses around the neighborhood: Tony Marindina's convenience store, Mr. Frank Feducia's barbershop, and Herby-K's, a bar and grill only a half block from my home. Past the bar and grill was a commercial area called West End, where you could find a drugstore, furniture store, movie theater, dentist office, bank, a Harley Davidson shop, clothing store, toy store, and an agriculture supply store.

From the drugstore, I would buy an occasional ice cream cone on holidays. Sometimes, I went to see a horror or western movie on Saturday morning at the movie theater, but I got nothing from the toy store. Nothing. I learned the cottage industry of how to make my own toys.

My mother took me to the dentist once and only once. The dentist was Dr. Beauchamp, whose office was above the bank. The dental chair was inches from an open window with no screen, just enough room for him to slip by or for me to fall out. He was going to fill a cavity that had been causing me a great amount of pain. It was my first (and almost my last) visit to the dentist.

My mother was in the room with me when Dr. Beauchamp asked an unusual question, "Do you want me to deaden it?" I thought he was going to kill me! My parents were going to have me done in by a non-

Italian, an Americano! That's child abuse. "What happened to family tradition?"

Then the torture began. Dr. Beauchamp said; "Let me know when it begins to hurt." For the next eternity, he drilled as I tried to grab his hand. He held me down with one hand and drilled with the other. I swear I saw a Sears Craftsman label on his drill. Did *Sears and Roebuck* sell dental equipment?

The drill felt like a jackhammer making street repairs. My eyeballs were bouncing in their sockets like a Harlem Globetrotter dribbling exhibition. I tried to gaze at the wall to see if Dr. Beauchamp had a diploma. It felt like he didn't. Psychologists are correct when they say early experiences mold your outlook of the future. One of my friends became a dentist, and I still won't speak to him.

Once a month I would go to the barber shop for a visit with Mr. Frank. Mr. Frank would say, "How do you want it cut little goomba?" I was hoping he meant my hair and not my throat. Remember, he was Italian. I would suggest, "Just a little off the sides and top." Then he would proceed to cut it the way he wanted.

He would put warm shaving cream on the back of my neck, take out the dull straight razor, wipe it across a large leather strap, and shave away my hair and sometimes my skin. Then he would wipe away the soap and blood from the back of my neck, spin the chair around towards a mirror, and say, "How does that look?" The hair cut was all right, but sometimes I had blood on my shirt.

Our next door neighbors were the Culotta family. We would open our window, and they would open theirs, so we could sit by the open windows and talk for hours between the houses. They had three girls and a boy. The two younger girls, Frances and Lucille, were near my age. Another girl, Beatrice, was my brother's age, and the oldest boy, Peter, was in college.

One day there was an argument between Peter and his father. Peter ran outside and his father threw a 90 MPH potato and hit him in the head. Peter instantly fell to the ground motionless. Their mother, whom we called Mrs. Mary, yelled, "You killed him! You killed our son!" Their father, whom we addressed as Mr. Sam, yelled, "*Thats agood!,"* and walked away. It was the classic Italian response to a family problem. Nothing personal, it was just being an Italian father.

What I remember most about my early neighborhood was that most residents were Italian, and they all knew each other. All of their homes were the same inside. Some icon of the Catholic religion and the aroma of Italian cooking permeated the confines of the walls.

My unmarried uncle (my mother's brother) lived with us in a back bedroom of our home. He was one of my favorite relatives because he knew so much about sports and would often attend sporting events and would bring home the game program.

Of course, his favorite teams became mine and they all had Italian players: Joe Di Maggio, Phil Rizutto, Roy Campanella, Carl Furillo, and Rocco Colavito. I liked the New York Yankees and the Brooklyn Dodgers because they had the most Italian players. He also dated some very attractive women.

He would order his lunch from Herby-K's and send me to pick it up. Although I was only five or six, I would walk in and tell the bartender why I was there. It was always very cool inside even in the hot summer. It was also rather dark, illuminated only by the glow of neon lights on the bar. The bottles of liquor with their fancy labels looked like decorations to me.

The patrons were all drinking and laughing and having a pleasant time. I wanted to be like them one day. As I picked up my uncle's sandwich, the bartender would always say, "Tell Sam hello, and you come back, little goomba." Little goomba was an Italian term of affection. That made me feel good, and it was a good business practice. Wal-Mart even has a greeter to make you feel welcome. "Welcome to Wal-Mart, little goomba." When I returned home, my uncle would reward me with a tip and a sip.

My uncle was also a boxer. He had a small scar on his chin. I was talking with him one day and asked him how he got the scar. He told me a tale only a naive kid like me would believe. (In school they taught me everyone was honest like George Washington!)

He said when he was a baby he was eating with a knife and missed his mouth. The tale finally ended when he said, "That's how I learned to eat and to fight with a knife." He also gave me advice that no parent would give a child.

A few days before school was out one summer, we had a class discussion just before the three o'clock bell. The teacher told us to tell how we would spend the first day of summer. The teacher would call on each student, and we took turns telling our plans to the class. One of my tormentors sat in front of me and said he was going swimming as soon as school let out.

I had never been swimming in a swimming pool, but it sounded good. When it was my turn to express my plans, I also said I was going swimming. The antagonist cut in, saying, "My dad said Italians can't swim in the public pool because they leave a dirt-ring around the edge."

Everyone laughed, and the teacher admonished them to get quiet. It was too late. I hung my head so my classmates couldn't see the tears forming in my eyes. I kept my head down until the bell sounded and everyone had left the room. The teacher asked if I needed any help, and I said no. I walked home in an ashamed daze. It was the first time my Italian heritage had been ridiculed by someone at school.

When I arrived, my uncle was the only one home. He sensed something was wrong and tried to cheer me up. He said, "Giovanni, do this" and smiled. (Whenever he called me by my Italian name, he was making an extra effort to be nice). "Do you feel sick?" he said. I answered with a soft, "No." Then he kept on, "What is it? Did your wife leave you?" This time I answered by shaking my head no.

After a pause, I told him what had happened at school. I could see his emotions turn from comical to serious. He asked, "Did it hurt your feelings?" This time I nodded yes. Unforeseen, he said, "Then you have to hurt him." It was the answer I wanted to hear.

I asked, "How?" Without hesitation he said, "Go punch him in the face." Wavering a bit, I said, "I don't want to get in trouble." Relieving me of that thought, he affirmed, "The police won't put you in jail; you're too young."

Demonstrating his boxing techniques, he instructed, "Spread your feet shoulder width for good balance. Keep both hands up to punch and defend punches." He continued, "Move your body side to side and slide your feet around like you're dancing. Your feet are as important as your hands. Good boy, now jab with your left hand, jab, jab, jab. The left jab sets everything up in a fight. Now feint with your left and hit with your right."

We practiced the movements on the kitchen floor. He sat me down and coached me on the mental approach. "Clear your mind of everything around you. Concentrate only on your opponent and his movements." Now I had some summer plans other than swimming. I had to find my tormentor and destroy him.

I walked to school the next morning, and there he was on the playground. I waited a moment and practiced my fight movements. Then I mentally prepared myself for the win. I walked up to him without saying a word and got in my fighter's stance. He laughed and said, "Do you wanna fight?" I started pumping left jabs at his face. The students on the playground backed off and exalted, "Fight! Fight!"

He retreated backward from my jabs, and I feinted a punch toward his stomach, and he dropped his hands. I saw an opening and threw an overhand right landing squarely on his left eye. I could hear the squish sound of my fist on his face. He bent over and put his hands over his eye.

The teachers on duty were walking quickly toward me. I still had time to throw more punches, but I didn't. He looked at me through his reddened and swelling left eye. I said, "Tell your dad this Italian left a ring around your eye."

Off to the principal's office we went. I told my story of why I had done it. I got the standard lecture of reporting a problem to the teacher rather than fighting. My teacher saw what had happened the day before. Nevertheless, I was given an early out for the summer. I went by my class and apologized to my teacher. As I walked home, I was glad for what I had done.

When I told the story to my mother and father, I got mixed results. My mother told me I should never fight. She said, "If you pray, the hurt feeling will go away." I got in trouble with my father, but not for fighting. He said, "You should have took care of his ass in class when he said it." It was the nicest thing he ever said to me. Well, you can't please everyone.

Later that night, my uncle came home from work. I went to his room and I told him what happened. He held my hand triumphantly up in the air. He smiled his approval and then whispered, "You didn't tell your mother I had anything to do with it, did you?" With a smug look, I said, "I didn't need your help." I knew I had just made an "A" in Italian 101; get even with your enemies and don't rat on your friends. I felt better about being Italian but just for a little while. I didn't want to be superior, I just wanted to be equal.

My uncle tried his best to explain to me why being Italian was different at that time. He told me if an Italian man did something good, like Joe DiMaggio, he would get the praise. Conversely, if an Italian man did something bad, like Al Capone, all Italians would get the blame. Continuing, he said, "When they say, 'May the best man win', they don't always mean it." After that talk, I didn't have a chip on my shoulder. Instead, I had the whole boot of Italy to defend.

3. Who was chosen as the most famous Italian American of the twentieth century?
   A) Al Capone
   B) Joe DiMaggio
   C) Frank Sinatra

The Lord helps me;
Therefore I have not been disgraced;
Therefore I have set my face like flint,
And I know that I shall not be put to shame
Isaiah 50:7

History to me has always been more than what happened and when it happened. I always wanted to know why it happened. Every historical event has a reason.

In the 1950s, boxing was a major sport and many Italians were professional fighters. My family, along with countless others, watched the "Gillette Friday Night Fights" every week on television, featuring Joey Giardello, Rocky Graziano, Jake LaMotta, Willie Pastrano, Carmen Basillio, and of course the only undefeated heavyweight champion in boxing history, Rocky Marciano. I'm proud of that list because I'm Italian. Personally, however, I think Muhammad Ali is the best boxer I ever saw. If Rocky Marciano and Muhammad Ali fought, Ali would probably win. Though I like both fighters, I would be for Marciano, whereas most, or all, African Americans would be for Ali. I call it ethnic human nature. There is nothing wrong with that.

The same Italian influence was evident in 1950s baseball. Many first generation Italians gravitated toward sports to find their "American Dream." Many Italian players dotted the rosters of major league baseball teams. Johnny Antonelli, Yogi Berra, Roy Campenella, Gino Cimoli, Rocco Colavito, Tony Conigliaro, Bobby Del Greco, Joe DiMaggio, Dominic DiMaggio, Carl Furillo, Tito Francona, Jim Fregosi, Joe Garagiola, Joe Pepitone, Rico Petrocelli, Vic Raschi, Phil Rizutto, John Romano, and Joe Torre.

Why were so many Italians in the 1950s involved in sports, entertainment, or crime? Maybe since they were a minority, they thought it was the most plausible way to "make it" in America. Connect the dots: minorities, sports, entertainment, and unfortunately, crime. Are these related?

The situation still exists today. Like it or not, understand it or not, accept it or not, agree or disagree, minorities don't feel as if they will ever get a fair chance in America. The fastest way for minorities to be accepted is through those channels. Those channels are not available to all minorities, except for crime. If they can help win a game, or if they can entertain, their ethnicity becomes less important to others. When minorities gain some sort of acceptance, they try to use their earnings or fame for the rest of their life. Minorities perceive the world differently.

I just want to know why minorities gravitate to these means. Minorities live their lives carrying the boot, the chains, and the reputations of their ancestors on their shoulders. Lack of acceptance is a difficult thing to live with, and trusting others does not come easy. Ethnicity can sway you to make unreasonable decisions, because minorities feel as if they must defend the honor of their parentage in all situations.

Other minorities in America have undergone much worse discrimination than I, but I can understand a portion of their anger, frustration, and mistrust. The good news is, as each generation passes, there has been progress toward unity. Many of my generation of Italian friends and relatives are married to non-Italian men or women. Their children are less ethnic in appearance and are more assimilated into society.

I don't carry any dislike for the prejudicial remarks I heard as a youth. Those people were speaking what they perceived as correct. It has taken me a lot of prayer, religious reading, and one-on-ones with Jesus Christ to accept what people say and to understand that I don't have to compare myself to others. I am who I am. Neither rhinoplasty nor hair relaxer was needed for this curly-headed Italian boy. I like my ethnic look…now.

Minorities are very proud of historical events in which they play a major role. The first African-American Justice of the Supreme Court was Thurgood Marshall in 1967. The first Italian-American Justice of the Supreme Court was Anthony Scalia in 1986. The first Hispanic Justice of the Supreme Court was Sonia Sotomayor in 2009. Should their ethnicity matter more than their beliefs about the Constitution? Are they token appointees? Some say yes, others no, and many don't even recognize the names.

Chapter 4
The Influence of Television

In the 1950s, television was the rage. I would stand outside on the sidewalk and watch television through Mrs. Brocato's picture window. Finally, she felt sorry for me and would invite me in some afternoons and would serve me Kool-Aid and a cookie. I then realized that television was much better with sound. I thought, "This invention is here to stay."

Eventually, my father broke his radio addiction and bought a television set for our family. It had one channel that broadcast from 8 A.M. until 10 P.M. I would watch whatever was on, even a blank screen.

Today my television set has over one hundred channels, and sometimes I can't find anything to watch. How we have changed. We have gained in technology, but we have lost in bonding with our family and friends.

Family television time is no more. Today, each family member often has his or her own room with a personal flat screen. Can you imagine an episode of *Father Knows Best* where Kathy is on Facebook, Bud is watching porn, Betty is at a motel with her boyfriend, Jim is watching Monday Night Football, and Margaret is watching a Lifetime movie about why you should not trust anyone in your family.

4. What television family of the 1960s was truly a real-life family?
   A) The Anderson family of *Father Knows Best*
   B) The Cleaver family of *Leave It to Beaver*.
   C) The Nelson family of *The Adventures of Ozzie and Harriet*.

By the end of the 1950s, the small black and white television set sat in living rooms across the country. We owned a Hoffman Console in 1954. Reception was brought to the screen by a set of "rabbit ears," Martian-looking antennae with two adjustable metal rods attached to a base and a wire that connected to the back of the television set. The rabbit ears also served as goal posts for my in-house football games, where I could kick a pair of rolled up socks through the uprights with accuracy.

Our city had one station, KSLA Channel 12. Later on, two other stations joined in, KTBS Channel 3 and KTAL Channel 6. At the closing of the viewing day, each station would play "The Star Spangled Banner." We would watch until the last note sounded and wake up early the next day to look at the test pattern. The test pattern was shown when no active program was playing. It was a picture of circles and lines used to fine tune the different shades of white, gray, and black.

5. What figure appeared in early television test patterns?
   A) Cowboy
   B) Indian Chief
   C) Bald Eagle

One Saturday morning, before the rest of the family was awake, I went into the living room and turned on the television set. Although no program was on, turning it on was a thrill because I was told not to touch it. There were three controls on the Hoffman: horizontal, vertical, and contrast. I turned the knob labeled "contrast" to the left and the screen became darker and darker until nothing could be seen. I panicked and hurriedly went back to bed.

Realizing I had done something wrong to our television set, I went outside to play the next morning. From outside, I heard my father screaming and cursing at the set. I started crying because I knew that I had broken our most valuable household item.

Immediately, my parents knew I was the culprit. I wanted to confess, but I thought my life was in danger. When they asked me what I had done, I walked up to the contrast control and turned it slowly to the right and the picture miraculously appeared. Everyone laughed, and I promised never to touch the television set again. I broke my promise later that day.

When the networks began televising sporting events, athletics became very popular in our culture. From that old Hoffman television set, I saw first-hand sporting events that are now called classics.

My first favorite was the 1955 World Series. The New York Yankees had been a dominant team in baseball, but the Brooklyn Dodgers won the Series in seven games. The final game was a 2-0 shutout pitched by Dodger lefthander, Johnny Podres.

Another event that I remember well was the 1957 World Series when the Milwaukee Braves beat the New York Yankees in seven games. My dear mother let me skip school for the last game, so I saw Lew Burdette shut out the Yankees in game seven, 5-0. I remember the game, but I would have never remembered anything from school that day. Great decision Mom!

One of my favorite players of the '57 Braves was a young outfielder from Mobile, Alabama, by the name of Henry Aaron. "Hammerin' Hank" became the all-time home run leader with 755 until his record was surpassed by Barry Bonds with his steroid-assisted 762. Hank could crank without performance-enhancing drugs. My Hank Aaron action figure still hangs on the wall above my computer. There's no room in my shrine for Barry Bonds. I also hope there's no room in the Baseball Hall of Fame for him.

In 1960, I watched a young Cassius Marcellus Clay Jr., win a boxing gold medal for the United States in the Rome Olympics. He became the heavyweight champion of the world in 1964, defeating Charles "Sonny" Liston. One day after the fight, Clay changed his name to Muhammad Ali. He became a cultural icon and social activist which led to his being idolized and vilified at the same time.

On a Sunday afternoon, in 1958, I watched what is called "the greatest game ever played." The Baltimore Colts defeated the New York Giants 23-17 in the first ever overtime football game to win the NFL Championship. The Colts were quarterbacked by the legendary Johnny Unitas.

After each of these sporting events, I would go outside and reenact what I had seen. I was Johnny Podres, pitching against the Yankees. I was Hank Aaron, hitting a homerun in the World Series. I was Cassius Clay, winning a three-round decision over a Polish fighter for the gold medal. I was Johnny Unitas, leading the Colts to the overtime win against the Giants. I would play, announce, cheer, and celebrate just as I had seen on television. I even interviewed myself.

My favorite television program as a child was the *Mickey Mouse Club*, a children's variety show created by Walt Disney. At the conclusion of the opening song, the host would say, "Mouseketeer roll call! Count off now......Sharon ....Bobby.........Lonnie........Tommy ....Annette.........Darlene..........Cubby.........Karen........Doreen........Roy ....Jimmie."

The show had a newsreel, a cartoon, a serial, some musical talent, and a few comedy acts. The adult host was Jimmie Dodd, assisted by another adult, Roy Williams. The members wore white shirts with their name across the front and the trademark attire of Mouseketeer ears, adorned their head. The ears were merchandising's hottest item. A small felt beanie with two, round, over-sized, black mouse ears at the top.

The most popular Mouseketeers were Annette Funicello and Darlene Gillespie. They were also the most physically eye-appealing. I guess you could say they were in the early stages of "hot." I know of one young Italian boy that began to have really human thoughts about Annette. She activated my hormone control system, and I began my awkward ascent toward puberty.

6. What male co-starred with Annette in the "Beach" movies of the 1960s?
   A) Frankie Avalon
   B) James Darren
   C) Troy Donahue

My mother bought me some Mouseketeer ears. I took them to school to show the class. It was rainy that day, and we had to remain indoors for recess. We rearranged the desks to have room to play and socialize inside.

I cut the elastic band on my Mouseketeer hat and added some rubber bands to enlarge the length. I attached the Mouseketeer ears around my upper body with the two large ears protruding from my chest. Looking for a laugh, I said, "Hey class, look at me, I'm Annette." The girls giggled, and the boys (who also had human thoughts of Annette) attacked my ears ... uh, my hat ...uh, my chest. They began to pull on the ears of the hat. They all had a smiles on their faces.

Our teacher, a young beauty herself, came to my rescue. She took the Mouseketeer beanie from me. The aroused, hyperventilating boys began shouting, "Put on the ears, Mrs. Firestone! Put on the ears!!" The sly Mrs. Firestone put the beanie on the top of her head. The girls laughed, and the boys were dispirited. Honestly, Mrs. Firestone already had some great "ears."

Once, we were playing outside at recess when I dove for the kick ball and skinned my elbow when I hit the ground. Mrs. Firestone walked over and cradled me in her arms and kissed me on the forehead. She looked at my elbow and said it was going to be okay. She was right. I never thought of my elbow injury again, but I thought of Mrs. Firestone often. She then chided, "Don't be so reckless when you're playing." I went back to the game diving for every kicked ball hoping for another injury and another kiss from Mrs. Firestone.

Through the wonders of television, my social life began to emerge. A major influence in early television was *American Bandstand.* The show gained nationwide popularity when Dick Clark took over as host on July 9, 1956. The show featured teenagers dancing to popular music. The guest spot was occupied by a recording artist who would lip sync his or her latest hit.

Clark would get teenagers' opinions about songs on a segment called "Rate-a-Record." They would rate the record, and I would rate the girl. Others were chosen for the "Spotlight Dance." They were not actors, just kids like the rest of us.

I really liked the show, and I noticed many teens with Italian names. They didn't try to conceal their ethnicity as I sometimes did. Today, I understand why. The teens lived in the Northeast United States heavily populated by Italian Catholics, and I was in the Baptist Bible Belt of the good ol' South. If I had lived in the Northeast, maybe I would not have felt so different.

My first-ever crush was on a teenage dancer named Carmen Jimenez. Her parallel would be the character Cha Cha DiGregorio in the movie *Grease,* remember, "the best dancer at St. Bernadette's." Carmen was the best dancer on *American Bandstand.* I could be with her every afternoon for an hour. She had an ethnic look, the classic curves, and the pouty lips that I liked.

However, my only contact with her was on the television screen and my imagination. When she danced, I would dance along, keeping an eye on the television set. I will never forget our first "Spotlight Dance" to *In the Still of the Night*. I held her close as we slow danced. After the dance, I was a distressed boy in love with a girl I could only see on the screen. What joy, what pain, what an imagination! I knew this relationship was not going to last. I needed to stop watching the show, but I couldn't. Carmen was my first broken heart. How do you mend a broken heart? You call Dr. Christiaan Barnard for a heart transplant.

7. What city was the location of the broadcast of *American Bandstand*?
   A) Los Angeles
   B) New York
   C) Philadelphia

8. Where did Dr. Christiaan Barnard perform the first human heart transplant in 1967?
   A) Cape Town, South Africa
   B) London, England
   C) Palo Alto, California

Many of the early television shows were adapted from popular old radio shows. Programs of the 50's and 60's grouped all viewers into one targeted group; white middle-class America. Discussing the topics of sexuality and race were taboo. Even the relationship of husband and wife characters was altered. On *The Dick Van Dyke Show*, husband, Rob Petrie (Dick Van Dyke), and wife, Laura Petrie (Mary Tyler Moore), had twin beds in the couple's bedroom. Was he always in the doghouse?

A groundbreaking controversial show appeared in the fall television season of 1968. *Julia* was an American sitcom notable for being one of the first weekly series to depict an African-American woman in a leading role. The star of the show was actress Diahann Carroll. Even Ms. Carroll remarked that the show was unrealistic. Critics claimed the show was a far cry from the actual lives of African-Americans in America, and the series was cancelled in 1971.

9. What was the first African-American television show?
   A) *The Jefferson's*
   B*) Different Strokes*
   C*) Amos 'n Andy*

In 1956, the quiz show, *Twenty-One*, damaged the credibility of all quiz shows on television. Charles Van Doren, an assistant professor of English at Columbia University, confessed before the United States Congress that he had been given the correct answers by producers of the show. The ploy was to boost the show's ratings. Television is always about ratings. Is it common practice for the entertainment industry to deceive the public in the quest for ratings? I survived with low ratings. In 1994, the movie, *Quiz Show*, was about Van Doren's role in the scandal.

Cheating takes place in all facets of life. It is probably an acceptable practice by many. Later on, during my career as a teacher, cheating was the thing that pissed me off the most. It is being lazy, dishonest, and disrespectful. Most teachers are willing to help any student if they are giving his or her best effort and fall short. Whether it was coaching football, or teaching in the classroom, I would always reward students or players if they were trying hard to succeed. I could always find a place for them.

There was a very beautiful and popular young girl in my American History class. Her class schedule must have read: first block, Make-up and Appearance; second block, Popularity Techniques; third block, Gossip and Fun; and fourth block, Rest and Recovery.

She often missed class on test day and relied on her many friends for help. Sometimes, she even tried to use her good looks on the teacher. Once, she told me I was handsome. Not meaning it, I responded, "I hear that all the time before a test." I didn't want her to think she could play me for a grade. Growing irritated by her laziness and conniving, I set up a sting.

She came to my desk to schedule a make-up test. At the time, I was grading another make-up test and she knew it. I made an excuse to go outside, and I left the answer key on the desk, knowing she would copy the answers. After giving her enough time, I re-entered the room.

We scheduled the test for the next day. She began proclaiming how she was going to study all night and make an "A." Later that day, I rearranged the questions-- same test, same answers, just in a different order.

She entered class the next day, telling me how much she had studied and learned. For emphasis, she even added how much she now liked history. It was classic cheating overkill. She completed the test and told me she knew all of the answers. She was right, but she didn't know what questions they answered.

I called her up to the desk to watch me grade her paper. Playing along, I said, "Let's see if your hard work paid off." She watched as I began to mark every answer wrong. She knew she had been taken.

I told her, "I don't understand. You have all of the correct information but with the wrong questions. If this were the original make-up test, you would have made a perfect score." Not willing to give in, she gave me the "You S.O.B look" and walked away. As she walked out of the room, I added, "Does this mean I'm not handsome anymore?" We never spoke again, and she failed the remainder of the semester. However, she did learn a lesson; education is not always what you learn from a textbook.

Chapter 5
The Music in Me

On Saturday nights, my policeman father would work security at the Louisiana Hayride held at Shreveport's Municipal Auditorium on Grand Avenue. Grand Avenue was renamed Elvis Presley Boulevard, based on one of Elvis's early performances in October, 1958. Ironically, our high school graduation was held at the Municipal Auditorium.

There was a stage drummer named Dominic Joseph Fontana that played with the house band. He lived down the street from my house, so I would often see him walking to the bus stop on the corner. He later gained fame as the drummer for Elvis Presley. He became D.J. Fontana, and I recognized him in many of the Elvis movies.

Another local musician and member of the stage band at the Louisiana Hayride was James Burton. Burton was a guitarist that played with Rick Nelson from 1958-1967, and later with Elvis from 1969 until Elvis's death in 1977. Burton was later inducted into the Rock and Roll Hall of Fame.

My mother, brother, and I would sit and watch the show. The best part of the show for me was watching my mother enjoy the music. She didn't have enough joy in her life.

My mother and father liked country music like most people of the city, but not me. We saw some great performers, Hank Williams, Johnny Cash, and Johnny Horton. The Hayride was second in popularity to the Grand Ole Opry in Nashville, Tennessee. It was billed as the "Cradle of Stars," and most became stars later in their careers. Once they gained popularity at the Hayride, they would move on to Nashville.

10. When Elvis first appeared on the *Ed Sullivan Show,* what stipulation was made by host Ed Sullivan?
    A) He had to cut his hair and shave his sideburns.
    B) He was required only to sing a ballad, no rock and roll.
    C) Television cameras could only show him from the waist up.

My parents would often dial the radio to KWKH, the country music station that broadcast the Louisiana Hayride live and played country music all day and night. The music style that I preferred then was R&B and Soul, and I never was sure which one I liked most. When I had possession of the radio, I would find a station that had some great Louisiana musicians.

One of my early favorites was Lloyd Price from Kenner, Louisiana. He put out four great songs: *I'm Gonna' Get Married, Personality, Question,* and *Stagger Lee*. The beat and sound of big band music is still my favorite. Antoine Dominique "Fats" Domino from New Orleans was known mainly for his signature hit *Blueberry Hill*, but he had many other delights, some of which are *Ain't That a Shame, Hello Josephine*, and *I Want To Walk You Home*. He also was of the big band rock era.

Cookie and the Cupcakes out of Lake Charles, Louisiana, hit it big with their classic *Mathilda*. Elton Anderson, also from Lake Charles, captured me with *The Secret of Love*. Another Lake Charles vocalist that I enjoyed was John Phillip Baptiste, musically known as Phil Phillips. He had a smash hit, *The Sea of Love*.

From Ponchatoula was the "Soul Queen of New Orleans," Irma Thomas, who sang my favorite, *I Wish Someone Would Care.* From Monroe, Louisiana, Toussaint McCall crooned *Nothing Takes the Place of You.* The soulful New Orleans native Aaron Neville, with a distinctive mole above his right eye, sang *Tell It like It Is* in 1967.

My non-Louisiana favorites were Billy Bland's, *Let the Little Girl Dance* and Ron Holden's, *Love You So*. These songs still play regularly at my house just for me. In fact, I want to listen to them now, so the "Do Not Disturb" sign is about to be placed on my door. I hope the neighbors like this music? These sounds make a connection with me. When I listen to this music, I never grow old. I become so excited, I have an eargasm!

Here I sit, gray and old
Listening to the sounds of gold
Johnny-Giovanni

Here are some accolades for my other favorites: Etta James, Otis Redding, Percy Sledge, Solomon Burke, Major Lance, James Carr, Sam Cooke, James Brown, Jerry Butler, Clyde McPhatter, O.V. Wright, and Ben E. King.

When it comes to singing *At Last*- sorry, Beyonce'- but Etta is "betta." Otis Redding's music could be classified as sermons on love. I wish everyone could hear Otis as I do. I *gotta, gotta, gotta* listen to Otis. (By the way, Otis and I have the same birthday, September 9.) If today's imitators met Percy Sledge, they would seek mercy from Percy. Solomon Burke was all heart and soul. Major Lance was *Um, Um, Um, Um, Um, Um*, gooooood... James Carr can still drive it home. You can't go wrong with O.V. Wright. Sam Cooke's sound was so sweet they listed the number of listening calories on the label. Dance moves? James Brown wears the crown. He is "The Godfather of Soul." "The Hardest Working Man in Show Business," Jerry Butler a.k.a "The Iceman," is classic old school, so his songs come with an automatic replay button. Ben E. King is so good he should just be King Ben.

I'm glad I grew up with this music, which nurtured the emotions and feelings I had for all my girlfriends. Sex was not a requirement to be in love with someone. Being "in love" is a very powerful emotion in itself, and I still cherish it today. When I listen to old music today, I am transported in a vinyl time machine which drops me off free of charge back to my teen years. Happy days are here again. They were classic songs to car-dance to. I still have my turntable, and the albums have been happily in and out of their covers for over fifty years. In my younger years, I spent a lot of leisure time listening to and imitating these performances, a major fascination to me. They helped me grow up and respect women, and today, I consider them close friends that I have never met.

Add to the list the legendary rocker Chuck Berry, who defined the rock and roll attitude; the great voice of Darlene Love; the super talented, Mary Wells; flamboyant Little Richard; the northern soul of the Tams; the sexy sound of the Supremes; the harmonizing compatibility of the Shirelles; soul sister number one, Aretha Franklin; and the raspy voice of Ray Charles singing *You Don't Know Me*.

One of my favorite male groups was The Drifters. (Every husband should play *This Magic Moment* every day for his wife.) My other choice is The Four Tops, with lead singer Levi Stubbs. How can I describe the indescribable? God's voice must sound like Levi's. My favorite female group was the Ronettes. I would often daydream of the young, lovely Veronica Bennett, who later became Ronnie Spector. I have read her biography, *Be My Baby,* three times, and I am saddened that my daydreams of her are not included.

11. Who was the first African American singer to have his own musical television show?
    A) Nat King Cole
    B) Little Richard
    C) James Brown

Two local bands received some national attention during my high school years. First, The Uniques with lead singer Joe Stampley from Springhill, Louisiana, became a local phenomenon. They played many early shows in Arkansas, Texas, and Louisiana. Later, Joe Stampley became a well-known country singer. I personally liked all of their music and still have their original albums. My two favorites, *All These Things* and *Strange*. Many young men probably got laid because of *All These Things*, me not included.

Another local favorite was John Fred and the Playboys, from Baton Rouge. They had a national hit, *Judy in Disguise,* but I personally liked *How Can I Prove?* and *You're On My Mind*. Just like I kept the albums from *The Uniques,* I have my original *John Fred and the Playboys* albums from the 1960s. Both *The Uniques* and *John Fred and the Playboys* recorded locally for Jewel Records, owned by Stan Lewis.

Stan Lewis began by opening the most popular record store in the area in 1948, Stan's Record Shop. It was called "the biggest little record shop in the South." Every teenager from the surrounding area bought their music from Stan "the Record Man" Lewis in the 1960s. It was also a place to see some beautiful young ladies.

There were two historical landings in the 1960s. Neil Armstrong landed on the moon on July 20, 1969, and The Beatles landed at JFK International Airport in New York on February 7, 1964. Which was the most historical?

Two days after they landed, The Beatles appeared on the *Ed Sullivan Show* before a record number of television viewers. That night was a life-changer for many. *Yeah! Yeah! Yeah!* There was a feeling that something special was happening. I liked their music and their personalities except for one, Paul McCartney.

Paul became the favorite of most fans, especially the girls. In my unprofessional opinion, he was using the band more than being a part of the band. From that night and until today, my evaluation is as follows: John, brilliant; Ringo, cool; George, reserved; and Paul, fake.

Americans welcomed Beatlemania and wholeheartedly embraced the British Invasion. Young boys grew their hair longer and faked British accents. The Beatles were singing what every boy was feeling. Most boys, including me, wanted to be the fifth Beatle. That's why I often display an early picture of myself with long hair and a mustache. I saw the world through the lenses of John Lennon's glasses and the lyrics of the songs he composed.

My personal choices of the best Beatle's music were the songs from the years 1963-1966. John wrote the majority of the songs and sang lead most of the time, though Paul claims that his contributions were equal. Get real, Paul. Does Paul even know that John was the founder of the group?

The Beatles broke up in 1970, and two of the four are alive today, Paul McCartney and Ringo Starr. John was murdered outside the Dakota apartment building on December 8, 1980, in New York City. George died of lung cancer on November 29, 2001, in Beverly Hills, California.

John Lennon was both controversial and unusual. His politics and anti-war stance led to his investigation by President Richard Nixon, who wanted to deport him from the United States. He once made the remark that the Beatles were more popular than Jesus. He chose a relationship with Yoko Ono over the group and it led to their demise.

What amazes me is that John, the founder and leader of the band, let Paul sing the first two songs of their American debut on the Ed Sullivan show, *All My Loving* and *Till There was You*. John could sing better, play better, write better lyrics; yet as a good leader, he let the other members of the band also become popular. How much success would Paul, George, and Ringo have had if not for being a member of The Beatles? Beatlemania still thrives in my home.

Rolling Stone ranks John Lennon the fifth best singer of all time. Paul is ranked eleventh. I understand that lists are in the mind of the creator, but it is *Rolling Stone*. There are so many great songs in the early years of the Beatles, but this would be my get-acquainted list: (I wish I could technically remove Paul from these recordings.)

(1) *In My Life*
(2) *Help!*
(3) *Tell Me Why*
(4) *I Should Have Known Better*
(5) *Do You Want to Know a Secret?*
(6) *From Me to You*
(7) *Eight Days a Week*
(8) *Ticket to Ride*
(9) *Anytime at All*
(10) *You Can't Do That*

Honorable Mentioned :(*I Cry Instead, All I've Got to Do, Girl, I'll Be Back, Not A Second Time, No Reply, I Saw Her Standing There, I Call Your Name, Nowhere Man, Eleanor Rigby)*

Also, the Beatles cover of the songs *Please Mister Postman, Baby, It's You and Anna* are excellent. John sings lead on all of the them.

12. What original member of *The Beatles* was replaced by Ringo Starr?
   A) Pete Townsend
   B) Pete Best
   C) Eric Clapton

13. Who does *Rolling Stone Magazine,* list as the number one singer of all time?
    A) Aretha Franklin
    B) Ray Charles
    C) Elvis Presley

My other favorites from the British Invasion were The Animals, with their sometimes strange bluesy songs: *When I Was Young, Sky Pilot, We Gotta Get Out of This Place,* and, of course, *House of the Rising Sun.* The Kinks, another British band started by brothers Ray and Dave Davies, had a very creative sound which could be considered the beginnings of the punk genre. They had some great hits like *You Really Got Me Now, All Day and All of the Night,* and *Till the End of the Day*

Every generation's culture has its own music. Today, young people laugh at what I listen to, and I understand. Today's musical styles don't make a connection with me. I can't accept "hoe" and "bitches" as beautiful musical lyrics.

The music of the Sixties has a lot to do with keeping high school romances alive in memories. As I have said earlier, sometimes I listen to the oldies all by myself, and for a moment, I'm back in school sharing time with Marilyn, Shirley, Jan, Jack, Mitch, Don, and Thomas. When I sing along, I don't have the talent to be in tune, but I do have the heart, the love, and the soul I acquired by listening to the greatest era of music.

The words remind me, no matter how old I am, of a previous time in a friendly place with the ones I loved. The songs are so nostalgic they make me long for days gone by. People are only capable of these emotions during a number of teen years, so it's always nice to revisit these memories.

Chapter 6
A New Neighborhood

All things come to an end, and my father decided he wanted to be a home owner rather than a renter. Movin' on up! He purchased a home away from the friendly confines of "Little Italy"-- no Italian neighbors, no bar and grill, no front porch, and no hiding space under the house. It was a good thing I realized the new house was built on a concrete slab before my next escape from misfortune. The house, with only two bedrooms and a small yard, was actually smaller than our rental. We were most proud of the carport, some luxury at last.

I went to school and played their game
They would laugh at my Italian name
Socially I was much too shy
All I wanted was to say good-bye
Johnny-Giovanni

Along with the new house came a new school. My old school in the Italian section was good because there were some Italians there and my older brother had blazed the trail, so the teachers knew my name and my family. The new school was a problem. I was scared and I didn't like it. Even on picture day, as I waited in line for my turn, I feared what the photographer might do. Before every picture he would say, "Smile," followed by a click of the camera shutter. I was thinking smile, click, smile, click and for me, "cry" click.

Elementary school was torture. I felt like I was the other kind of American who had dark curly hair with a foreign name sitting in a class with straight-haired kids with normal names. Thank God my mom dropped the Giovanni from my name when she enrolled me.

Few teachers or students could pronounce my name correctly. They didn't even try. When the teacher called roll at the beginning of class and my name was mispronounced, everyone would laugh and call me that "funny" name the rest of the day. Mine was the only name the class listened for during roll call. Therefore, from the beginning of class until the final bell, I became an introvert.

You know how some people run away from home? Once, I ran away from school. We were taking our afternoon break from class. On Thursdays, we would march to the cafeteria where students were able to buy an Eskimo Pie or Popsicle for five cents. I stayed in line, but I never had the five cents. I would just pass by and say, "No, thank you."

One Thursday, I grew tired of this humiliation, slipped out of line, and went home. Either no one saw me, or no one cared. When I got home, I told my mother we had gotten out of school early. The telephone rang minutes later, and it was the school principal looking for me. My mother confirmed I was home. She tried to get me to confess what was wrong, but I could not tell anyone. They would probably just laugh again.

Daily recess in the sun
I could throw, catch and run
What I learned in the end
It was the way to make a friend
Johnny-Giovanni

At recess, my popularity grew. Everyone wanted me on their team, because they knew I could help them win. Somehow, they learned how to pronounce my name when it was their turn to choose, so I found a way to survive. I gained plenty of confidence once my classmates accepted me. To my surprise, even the girls wanted to carry my baseball glove or wear my jacket during the game. A couple of girls even asked if they could straighten my hair.

Athletics is still that way today. Crowds of people and beautiful women gravitate toward athletes. Just check out the wives and girlfriends of some professional athletes. Athletes get respect for being athletes, not for the person they are. That is a problem.

The most traumatic incident during my early years did not happen at school, however, but at the University Medical Center. When I was nine years old, I was playing at my grandparent's house. The sun was setting, and I saw a stray kitten. I picked the kitten up and put it near my face so I could look at it closely. The kitten swatted me with its right paw, scratching me under the left eye. I showed my mother the scratch; she cleaned it, and we didn't think about it anymore.

After about two weeks, however, I started having a high fever and headaches. Then came the worst of all symptoms. My testicles swelled to twice their normal size, and they were very painful. (No luck in the other appendage getting larger.) Compared to my testicles, my penis looked like a pencil eraser. I was totally out of proportion in the critical manhood area.

There was too much discomfort and pain for me to walk. My mother called my pediatrician, and I was off to the most terrible, painful, humiliating examination I've ever had. Two nurses held my legs spread open while the doctor probed and squeezed my genitals. I was screaming, crying, and trying to recall the mortal sin I must have committed to deserve this.

The doctor produced a camera and took several pictures of my enlarged testicles and my minuscule "eraser." Where would these pictures end up? Didn't he need my permission to show them? Could I buy them back? Would my classmates see them? Was he going to sell them to the *National Enquirer*? What headline would the magazine use?

I was filled with fear. He sent us home and said he was going to consult with some other doctors and he would call us later.

The next day we received the call saying he wanted to see me again. The diagnosis was a rare condition called inoculation lymphoreticulosis, also known as cat scratch disease. The disease can be classified as classical or atypical. No doubt I had the atypical strain.

Symptoms are headaches, fever, pain, swollen lymph nodes or glands. Recovery time was two to four months. Each week, I went to the doctor for my photo shoot and testicle massage. The case was so rare they sent me to the medical school for show and tell. Doctors at the university hospital picked me up one morning from my house and transported me to a class of eagerly-waiting interns. After being rolled to class in a wheelchair, I stood on an examination table in front of the class.

That day's lecture was about me. The doctor opened my hospital gown like the curtains to a peep show. The class walked to the examination table for a close-up of the boy with the giant testicles. I had donated my body to science at age nine. They asked me some questions, and I answered all of them… with my eyes closed.

Since I obviously could not go to school, my elementary school arranged for my teacher to come by my house once a week to tutor me and leave me some assignments to work on at home. I also had the choice of dropping out of school for the term and repeating the fourth grade.

After three months, the fever, headaches, and swelling were gone. The only treatment I needed next was mental therapy. We made the last appointment with the doctor, and he gave me my release to return to school. We thanked him for his help, and he asked if there were any questions. I only had one. Where are those pictures? The doctor told me I was famous. My pictures would be in medical textbooks for doctors to learn about the disease. I prayed that they would not show my face or print my name.

14. Who released a song and album in 1977 titled *Cat Scratch Fever*?
   A) KISS
   B) The Who
   C) Ted Nugent

In my fifth grade class was a girl named Laura. Laura wore makeup and had the semblance of already having boobs. Laura already had a reputation that was a curiosity. It was said she was already dating high school boys. Some said she didn't wear panties to school. I looked closely, but I couldn't tell. One particular story was that while going to the restroom she saw a boy in the hall and took him into the dark empty auditorium and made out with him. I placed this story in my memory bank, and it was drawing compounded interest.

One day in class, Laura asked Mrs. Butler for permission to go to the restroom. I witnessed this because I sat in the front of the class at Mrs. Butler's request. I watched Laura, wearing a smile and a tight dress, and maybe panties, walk out of the room. Suddenly, I got a call from my memory bank. I was thinking if I could get out of class and walk up and down the hall near the auditorium, maybe Laura would take me into the dark vacant auditorium and make out with me. My heart was accelerating, and my imagination was churning out X- rated thoughts.

I stood up at my desk and asked, "Mrs. Butler, may I have permission to go to the restroom?"

She stared at me for a brief moment as if she was reading my mind and said firmly, "No." I stood there crushed and humiliated. Mrs. Butler said, "Johnny, I have heard the rumors also, and we are going to keep them just that, rumors." As I sat back down, I could only think that someone else was making out with Laura in the auditorium.

I was seated in front of Mrs. Butler not for academic achievement but for academic deviance. Our assignment was to write a statement and a question using each of our twelve spelling words. I thought of a brilliant solution to this lesson.

"Automobile" was the first word. For my statement I wrote, "I know what 'automobile' means." For my question, I put on my assignment, "What does 'automobile' mean?" I used this technique for all twelve words. I was so proud of my accomplishment! I even sold my method for ten cents to my classmate, Keith.

When Mrs. Butler read our papers and learned of the scam, she called Keith and me to her desk and wanted one of us to confess. He blamed me, and I blamed him. Keith then said, “I paid him ten cents for his answers.” Mrs. Butler had us empty our pockets. Keith didn’t have any money, but I had a dime. Crime just seems to follow Italians around.

Some of the new neighborhood boys thought it was cool to make fun of Italians. The jokes and insults didn’t bother me if they came from my friends. The word that irritated me most, however, was the incorrect pronunciation of “Italian,” such as “Are you Eye-talian?” or “I like Eye-talian food.” To make matters worse, they were all spoken with a southern accent.

Nevertheless, it is great being a specific ethnicity in America. I had friends with the family names of Ladatto, Felan’, Martinez, Bindo, Maranto, and Tuminello. Some neighbors gave us what they thought were cool insults like “Wop,” “Pineapple,” and “Taco.” We anointed the neighborhood white boys with lame nicknames such as “Fatso,” “Cry Baby,” or the one I learned in school, “White Anglo-Saxon Protestant,” or just “WASP.”

My Italians buddies and I would say, “Go back to your nest, WASP,” or “I’m going to spray you with some Raid.” These were not much of an insult, but remember, we were only seven or eight years old. Today, that would be considered a slur or a hate crime. You could probably be booked on Dr. Phil and receive permanent disability payments for the rest of your life for the emotional distress it caused.

It was amusing when people thought they could befriend us with an Italian joke or a hokey Italian accent. Just like today, offensive words were all right if we said them to each other, but it was insulting to hear them from non-Italians. I don’t know why, but all ethnicities are like that. You feel the love from some insults, and others are just insulting.

Some of the more common names people call those of Italian descent are “Dago,” “Goomba,” “Greaseball,” “Guido,” “Guinea,” and “Wop.” I am all of the above and more. Just don’t call me “Eye-talian.” On the other hand, here is how these terms originated and what they basically mean.

“Dago”- Italian immigrants would work and be paid by the day (as the day goes).
“Goomba”- Godfather, implying Mafia connections or a slang term for a person of Italian descent.
“Grease ball”- an Italian man who slicks his hair back and the hair ointment runs down the side of his face
“Guido”- stereotype name for an Italian-American man
“Guinea”- Italians of dark skin color like the people of the African nation of Guinea
“Wop - “without papers,” an illegal Italian immigrant

Every Sunday in the fall, we played the weekly neighborhood football game. The gridiron was a vacant lot between two houses. The sidelines were marked by a row of bushes and a concrete driveway. The north end zone was a residential street, and the south end zone was an alley. Game time was from noon until dark, or until a fight broke out. We had some simple rules for safety. You couldn’t tackle on the sideline that was the concrete driveway. I broke that one all the time. It was the easiest way to hurt somebody. If you scored at one end of the field, you had to turn around and run back because our field was not long enough. And my personal rule, the game could not end if my team was behind.

One memorable game started and ended on the same play. The kickoff that started the game went from the south alley toward the north residential street. The kick sailed high and far into the air toward the street. A driver in a pickup truck was moving down the street, and the ball made a perfect landing in the back of the pickup. The unknowing driver never noticed or slowed down and drove off with our football. Game over. I learned right then, to play sports you had to have two balls, both kinds. From then on all kicks were toward the alley. These games had Hall of Fameless participants composed of neighborhood players:

Harold, a deaf mute, age thirty-two. The only position he could play was center because you couldn’t explain the play to him. Holding his hearing aid in his pocket, he would bend over the ball and look upside down through his legs. The quarterback would indicate the signals with his fingers. Silently, he would point with his fingers, one, two, or three. This was the beginning of the silent count in football. After Harold delivered the ball to the quarterback, he would stand and cheer. Sometimes he would argue after the play, but no one knew what he was trying to say. I verbally abused Harold at times, but, of course, he didn't hear me. Silence is golden. Sometimes, I would pretend to shout but not say anything. Harold would frantically try to adjust the reception on his hearing aid to no avail.

Paul was an eight year-old with a fungus growing on his head. We always had a rule it was a penalty if you touched Paul on the head. We would also add, "The doctor said the fungus might be contagious."

"Sis" was the name we gave to one teenage boy. It meant sissy because he played like a girl and would get injured on every play. According to us, he had no balls, but instead two vaginas. He had too many of his mother's genes to play football.

Jimmy was our quarterback. He was so intimidated by his own teammates he couldn't speak in the huddle. Because of this, he was usually my opponent when the fisticuffs (fights) started, even though he was my teammate.

Phillip was a star high school player who was bigger and better than any of us. Philip received a football scholarship to LSU after his senior season. I always tried to hurt him so he couldn't play on Friday night. I was never successful.

My Uncle Hunter, age thirty-one. He previously had knee surgery and used it as a scam. Every time I would prepare to tackle him, he would call time out and say his knee locked.

My cousin Jim was always on the opposing team. I didn't like him. The first time he played, he broke away and ran for what he thought was a touchdown. He didn't know the rule that you had to turn around and run back because of our short field. He yelled, "Touchdown!" I replied, "Touchdown my ass. You have got to run back." Revenge was mine.

Lloyd, age twenty-eight. He only played one game, and when he scored a touchdown on me, he quit, saying, "I have to go tell my wife I made a touchdown!" I shouted back, "Be sure and tell her you were playing against a ten-year old, you asshole."

Some players changed from week to week, but the outcome was always the same. Game called because of a fight, or if my team lost, my brother and cousin would hold me down so everyone could go home safely.

As I entered junior high school, I thought I was much more adjusted because of athletics. I played on a number of little league baseball teams and football teams and won a lot of ribbons at field days. I could name the starting lineup for the St. Louis Cardinals and their pitching rotation. I thought, "With those credentials, how could I fail in school?" Here's how:

In the seventh grade, I was tormented by a student in class. I sat next to him because we were seated in alphabetical order. He wore a black leather jacket, had sideburns and a ducktail, and as Forrest Gump might say, "He smelled like cigarettes." He had a striking resemblance to the Kenickie character in *Grease.* One day, he whispered to me, "When the teacher ain't looking, I'm going to wop you in the arm, Wop."

Stanley carried out his threat by hitting my arm and saying "Wop" every time he hit me. My arm hurt so much I thought I was going to have to become a lefty. We had physical education class together, and he was still carrying out his threat. He continued to hit me in the arm, *Wop, Wop, Wop*. In the locker room or in the gym, he kept his promise. Our physical education coach saw what was going on and asked if there was any trouble. Thinking the coach would make him stop, I explained the situation. Unfortunately for me, this coach must have been a hard-ass ex-Marine. He said, “Boys, here is how we will settle this.” He went to the coaches’ office and came back with two pair of boxing gloves. Of course, schools wouldn’t allow this today, but this was 1960.

The P.E. class gathered in a circle to form a ring in the gym. They were eager with anticipation to see me get my ass whipped. Maybe they would even see some blood or spaghetti sauce. I was full of both. The coach said we would fight for three minutes. He blew his whistle, and the bout was on.

Swinging wildly going for an early knockout, Stanley charged at me. I called it the windmill technique. His problem was that all he created was wind and a fatigued body in about thirty seconds. He was not going to survive the final two and half minutes without a cigarette break. All my training in the back seat of the ‘48 Dodge from avoiding my dad’s punches and the training from my boxer uncle began to pay dividends. I stayed calm and eluded him. He couldn’t lay a glove on me, and I hit him with a solid punch at every opening. Stanley got more frustrated, which created more openings. I dominated the fight. When the whistle blew after three minutes, I had won by a unanimous decision.

The class went wild. They carried me around the gym on their shoulders. It was an upset of epic proportions, and word spread throughout the school. The Italian boy could fight! I could hear the Mafia ghosts applauding and calling out, “We need this kid! Good job, Goomba.”

Remember in the movie *Rocky,* after the first fight when Apollo Creed said, *“There ain’t gonna be no rematch”* and Rocky answered, “*Don’t want one.”* Well, this was not the movies, and Stanley wanted a rematch, but not in the gym with boxing gloves. Stanley II was to take place in the parking lot with fists after school and no supervision to slow him down.

As the final school bell rang that day, I went to face the opening punch of the fight. Stanley was already in the parking lot. He had probably skipped his final class and smoked a few cigarettes to prepare for the fight. He did that on most days. The crowd gathered. What a memorable day, two fights between the same two people on the same day. *"A day that will live in junior high infamy,"* one student said.

I looked around trying to find any advantage I could. The parking lot was equipped with six-inch restraining curbs in front of each parking space to prevent the parked car from moving forward. Stanley was standing by one of the curbs as I approach him.

He was about four inches taller than me. He put up his fists in fight position, and I stepped up on the curb and dropped him with a sneak right hand. Howard Cosell would say, *"Down goes Stanley! Down goes Stanley!"* As he got to his knees, I hit him with another right hand. It was a cheap shot but effective. My confidence was soaring. I was ready to throw my next barrage of punches. A teacher in the parking lot ran over and stopped the fight. I celebrated a TKO in the first round. I really didn't want to fight anymore, but for some good public relations, I yelled, "Get up and let him go! I'm not finished with him!" Thankfully, they didn't let him go.

In my mind, I was immortalized with other great Italian boxing champions, Rocky Marciano, Jake LaMotta, Carmen Basilio, and Rocky Grazziano. The next day at school my reputation took flight. I was living the good life. Students offered me candy and gum, girls smiled, and I was suspended. I anointed myself "Two Time Johnny." Two wins in one day. Now I had a nickname worthy of my Italian brothers in the Mobster Hall of Fame. Stanley and I became friends for the rest of our school years.

One of my worst offenders was a corner neighbor named Leo. Anytime I went to the store or was on my way home, I had to pass Leo's house. His family ran a grave stone business in a shop behind their house. Some samples were set up in their yard which made it an eerie sight.

Leo seemed to have some kind of radar when I approached the corner. He had his array of welcomes like "Your name is gonna be on one these, boy" or "How much is it worth for you to pass my house, boy?" One fine summer day, he was outside watering the plants in his front yard. I thought I could walk by undetected, but his radar quickly responded to my movements. Leo said, "I'm gonna let you by this time, boy." He always would end his statements with "boy." As I proceeded along the sidewalk, he sprayed me with the water hose.

When I returned home dripping wet, I was disciplined for "ruining my clean clothes." No explanation would suffice. It was time to get even with Leo. I planned my first hit.

Leo had a fishing boat with a canvas cover on the side of his house. I gave my friend Carlo my BB gun and told him to hide under the canvas in the boat. I would walk by Leo's house, and when he threatened me, Carlo was to jump from under the canvas cover and shoot Leo with the BB gun. I discovered that there was a little Al Capone in these Italian genes.

I walked by in my new set of dry clothes, and there was Leo. As I approached his house, he grabbed the water hose and turned it on. I yelled to Carlo, "Now!" Carlo rose up out of the boat and pumped two BB's into Leo's back. I ran north and Carlo ran south, and Leo's head was on a swivel trying to find the culprit.

Remember, this is my life, and there was rarely a happy ending. My life was like Forrest Gump's without the success. I found a turtle and was keeping it in a box outside as a pet. One day my turtle was missing. I hoped it would be somewhere in the yard, but I couldn't find it. The turtle was back in the box the next day, nailed shut in his shell with the name Leo carved into the shell. That night, the turtle went to sleep with the fishes.

Chapter 7
Mafia Roots

The Mafia began in old Italy on the island of Sicily as an organization to protect people against the abusive government. The rules began there and came to America during immigration in the late 1800s and early 1900s.

Hard times led to new opportunities to make money, or "score some dough," through prostitution, extortion, and gambling. By the early 1900s, many progressives and traditionalists supported Prohibition. They believed the prohibition of alcohol would help reduce unemployment, domestic violence, and poverty. The Eighteenth Amendment was passed in 1919 and took effect in January of 1920. The new law prohibited the manufacture and sell of alcoholic beverages in the United States.This law handed the Mafia a new lucrative business. Bootleg liquor.

The bootleg liquor was sold in speakeasies. Organized crime specialized in supplying and running these illegal bars. Smugglers brought liquor into the United States from Canada and the Caribbean. Smuggling and consumption of liquor helped create an illegal billion-dollar industry for gangsters. Crime became big business and some mobsters had enough money to corrupt local politicians. Police officers, judges, and public officials were often on the payroll of gangsters. Al Capone made millions of dollars and controlled 10,000 speakeasies in Chicago. Many other crimes, including murder were linked to Capone. Prohibition became too violent and expensive to enforce.

15. What was a slang term for a speakeasy during the Prohibition Era?
    A) A Waterfront
    B) A Water Hole
    C) A Blind Tiger

16. What amendment eventually repealed the 18th Amendment?
    A) 19th Amendment
    B) 20th Amendment
    C) 21st Amendment

17. What crime was Al Capone convicted of and imprisoned for in 1931?
    A) Murder
    B) Income tax evasion
    C) Bribery of public officials

After Prohibition, New York became the next big Mafia city. Charles "Lucky" Luciano murdered his way to the top and became "The Boss" of New York.

The Mafia has also been connected to the Kennedy family. There were rumors that the Mafia provided Joseph Kennedy and his son, John Kennedy, with women. Some even say the Mafia helped John Kennedy get elected in the close presidential election of 1960. There was talk that the Mafia began to turn on the Kennedy family because they began to interfere in their organized crime business. Because of these reports there is a theory that the Mafia assassinated President Kennedy. Jack Ruby, who killed suspected presidential assassin Lee Harvey Oswald, was mentioned as a Mafia associate. As it often is in the Mafia, there is no solid evidence of these theories.

In my Old Italian neighborhood, "Little Italy," when we played cops and robbers, everybody wanted to be a robber. It was in our genes. The Mafia had such cool nicknames that it made you strive for a title: Tough Tony, Tony the Trigger, Joey Diamonds, Lucky, Mad Dog, Sam the Cigar, One-Eyed Pete, The Undertaker, Frankie the Wop, Little Vinny, Tony Pro, Frankie the Beast, and Tony the Ant. To a young Italian boy, these were terms of endearment.

When the *Untouchables* premiered on television in October of 1959, we pulled for Al Capone and Frank Nitti and detested government agent Elliot Ness. There was no harm intended, we were Italians. When the childhood game of cowboys and Indians was played on reservations, how many Indian boys wanted to be cowboys? Do you think Native Americans go to the movies and pull for the Cavalry? The Italian community of New York protested the show, saying it promoted negative stereotypes of Italians as mobsters and gangsters. I thought, "Not all Italians are mobsters and gangsters, just 90 percent. The other

10 percent are somewhat law-abiding citizens."

Hollywood romanticized the Mafia lifestyle in *The Godfather, Goodfellas, Donnie Brasco, A Bronx Tale, Casino, Once Upon A Time in America,* and *The Sopranos.* Many people have seen these productions and know the characters Don Corleone, Tommy DeVito, Lefty Ruggiero, Cologero "C" Anello, Nicky Santoro, Frankie Manoldi, and Bobby Baccalieri. Fans repeat the lines, *"I'm gonna make him an offer he can't refuse." "It's not personal; it's strictly business.,"* and the phrase *"Badda Bing!"*

The Godfather theme song, *Speak Softly Love,* has been listened to and sung by millions. As the music plays and Andy Williams sings, visions and feelings for Michael Corleone suggests those men were more than murderous Mafia businessmen. The romantic side of the culture was as exhilarating as the "hits." I prefer to be a romantic Italian. Andy Williams passed away on September 25, 2012 -- *riposa in pace*.

18. Who won the Academy Award for Best Actor in the 1972 film *The Godfather?*
    A) Marlon Brando
    B) Al Pacino
    C) Robert Duvall

Chapter 8
My "Big" Italian Family

A big Italian family consists of a lot of "bigs." There were big cars, big family gatherings, big appetites, big meals, big waistlines, big hugs, and big men with big noses. Big is not always good. At the weekly impromptu family reunions at my grandparents' home lived the legend of the big bosomed Italian woman. This was no optical illusion. If two well-endowed Italian women were in a room together, it was like four. You had to contort your body to move through the maze of bountiful bosoms. "Excuse me, Aunt Rosina." Again, "Excuse me, Aunt Rosina." (I thought I was already past her). That's how Italian men acquire affection for "big ones" at an early age.

However, these women also had some imperfections. They considered overweight anything more than three hundred pounds. Too many of these beauties on the family tree would uproot it. Most had a mole with a thick, black, crooked hair or two jutting out like the antennae on an insect. The hairs were so thick you could etch glass with them. You could also glimpse a few chin whiskers, a mustache, or some hairy legs and arm pits. You don't acquire an affection for those! You hope to acquire memory loss. Sadly, those big, strong, hairy Italian women are becoming fewer and fewer. Italians have married many non-Italians, and those dominant Italians genes have now been modified.

Our Aunt Rosina kept the heredity of big Italian women alive. The cousins nicknamed her "Big Wooly Mammoth." She was really like Queen Kong. One Christmas at my grandmother's house, we tried to convince Aunt Rosina to get on the roof of the house. We wanted to throw fireworks at her to see if she would growl and swat them away. A family rumor is there is a replica of her in the Smithsonian next to Tyrannosaurus Rex. Italian women are becoming extinct like the dinosaur. Thank God!

On the other hand, the young Italian beauties were celestial, physically mature beyond their young age; daring and dedicated to the men they pretended to love. On the flip side, some of those girls began shaving before I did; not their armpits or legs, but their chins.

One of my most unusual Italian relatives was my Aunt Mia. She was born in Italy. Her home was like old Italy. She had a font of holy water to the right of the front door, various religious statues and pictures in most every room. There was a small kitchen adorned with garlic pods and home-grown vegetables from the backyard garden covering the small counter, a sauce-stained apron hanging by the oven, and always a pot of spaghetti boiling on the stove. Only Italian was spoken in the home. What the hell did she come to America for?

The signature room of her home was a spare bedroom converted into a Catholic altar. A Catholic church right there in the house. Talk about a home make over. I always suspected if I opened the bedroom closet, a priest would be in there hearing confessions.

It was believed that Aunt Mia had special powers. She could dream the future and accurately predict the outcome of events. I tested her authenticity once by asking her who would win the 1958 World Series. I thought with her help, I might be able to pick up some extra lunch money at school. I was willing to give her 25% of the take. If it turned out she was good at this, maybe we could go into business together. I guess her powers didn't transcend into the world of sports. She didn't have a clue as to what I was asking. Maybe I should have asked in Italian?

Aunt Mia had a unique way of carrying on a conversation or working and reciting the Holy Rosary at the same time. Like a nun, she had a giant rosary attached to her waist at all times, and whatever she was doing, you could see her fingers moving from one rosary bead to the next. In the middle of a conversation, I would see her complete the rosary, make the sign of the cross with the crucifix, and still be talking to her family. She was bilingual in a religious way.

The first family death I remember was the sudden passing of Aunt Mia's husband. The relatives gathered at her house, which was standing room only. She was seated in the center of the room, dressed in all black and surrounded by Italian friends and relatives holding their rosaries. She led the prayers of the Holy Rosary, and everyone would follow. It was the ultimate form of respect and love.

Aunt Mia made some vows after the death of her husband. One was, she would wear black for the rest of her life, and another was she would visit and pray at her husband's grave site as frequently as possible. Both vows were maintained until her own death more than twenty years later.

Numerous times our telephone would ring, and after the conversation, my mother would say, "I have to go take Aunt Mia to the cemetery." At one family gathering, they were passing around photos of Aunt Mia at the cemetery. In the first picture, Aunt Mia was on her knees praying at the grave site of her deceased husband; picture two, Aunt Mia was making the sign of the cross at the grave site; picture three, Aunt Mia was lying across the grave. I didn't know what to expect next. In picture four Aunt Mia was holding a shovel! I didn't want to see picture five. No! No! Please Lord! Blind me! In picture six Aunt Mia was planting flowers. Thanks be to God! I have total respect and love for Aunt Mia, and I consequently forgave her for not picking the Yankees in seven games in the '58 World Series.

Uncle Nari and Aunt Concetta owned a small neighborhood grocery. They were living the American Dream of entrepreneurship and the free enterprise system. Well, there was a small miscalculation. The key words in real estate are location, location, location. You don't locate your store in a part of the city where the police are afraid to patrol. Unfortunately, they did, so they were often robbed.

To make matters worse, after each robbery they would call my father because after all he was on the police force. As a policeman, he would surely offer a kind ear and some safety advice before the next robbery. After all, the police motto was "To protect and serve." His motto was "To protect, serve, and humiliate." I was privy to one of the conversations, which went something like this:

Aunt Concetta: "He came into the store and said he had a gun."
My father: "Did you see the gun?"
Aunt Concetta: "No, he just said he had one and wanted the money from the cash register."
My father: "What did you do?"
Aunt Concetta: "I gave him the money."
My father: "Don't you know if he had a gun he would have shot the shit out of you. That's how stupid you are."

There was another episode at the store. Our phone rang, and Aunt Concetta said, "Come quickly to the store. There has been an accident!"

Uncle Nari had cut his finger using the meat slicer. We rushed to the scene and his hand was wrapped in a bloody towel. This was the conversation as I remember:

My father: "What happened?"
Aunt Concetta: "Nari was slicing some bologna, and his finger hit the slicer."
My father: "What did you do?"
Aunt Concetta: "I said, Blessed Mother, Blessed Mother, he cut his finger like the other!" (This was no time to start rapping Aunt Concetta.)
My father: "Well, Goddamn, how was that going to help?"

You could always take your problems to my dad and he would always make you feel worse. He never apologized. It was just that Old Italian belief of not showing sympathy. He wanted us to be tough. We accepted it without question. It was the least harmful of all the Old Italian beliefs.

Beautiful Carla, held my hand
We kissed to the music of Jerry Vale
As the New Year's confetti fail
And I became an adolescent man
Johnny-Giovanni

My uncle on my mother's side of the family lived in Dallas. He invited my cousin and me to the Cotton Bowl football game on New Year's Day. New Year's Eve night we all went out to celebrate. I had no knowledge of where we were going and my upbringing had taught me not to ask questions. We drove up to a rather large white building. The sign outside was painted with the words A-I Club.

Our party of four, my uncle, his friend, my cousin, and I, approached the door and knocked. A small speakeasy type window opened and then the door. There was crowd of about fifty people inside, a large bar tended to by a black man dressed in waiter's attire, loud Italian music playing maybe Jerry Vale or Dean Martin, a pool table with a crowd of men and some large bills on the table, beautiful women dressed in provocative gowns, and men sporting handguns holstered on the side on their chest. It was just a normal Italian New Year's Eve party.

Being law abiding and considerably under-aged, my cousin and I walked up to the bar and asked for a soft drink. The smiling black man asked us, "Do you want Coke or 7-Up?" My cousin and I looked at each other and said, "Coke." The bartender took two glasses from behind the bar and filled them halfway with ice and Coke. As we reached for the glasses, he filled the remainder with Jack Daniels. Let the party begin.

I did meet a pretty young Italian girl there named Carla. She smelled good and looked even better in a low cut, tight, red dress.

Things were looking up. The more we talked, the more I began to embrace my Italian culture and Carla. I will confess, she just wanted to talk but I wanted to jabber. Do you understand?

That one Jack Daniels and coke and Carla's body in that red dress was a lethal combination for my adolescent mind. My judgment was impaired and I became a hedonistic light-headed fool. As Jerry Vale rang in the New Year with his voice, Carla rang in my New Year's with a kiss, and not just a kiss, but a kiss the Beatles sang about. They were right; I never realized what a kiss could be. I had two thoughts, "How did she do that?" and "Please do that again!" Happy New Year became the Happiest of New Years. Finally, being Italian had an upside. Thank you, Carla, for my number-one kiss of all time. Also, how old were you?

The next day we went to the Cotton Bowl and watched LSU defeat Texas 13-0. I don't remember much about the game but I remember everything about the previous night with Carla.

Chapter 9
Surviving Catholicism

It was difficult as a young boy growing up in the Catholic faith. Being Italian was like you had two choices in life: be a priest or be in the Mafia. There was an allure to names such as Alphonse Capone, John Gotti, and Sam Giancana. There was also something special about Pope Pius XII (Giovanni Pocelli), Pope John XXIII (Guiseppe Roncalli), and Pope John Paul I (Albino Luciani).

Popes and parish priests were presented as heroes with their colorful clothes and mysterious rituals. They were all so cool. I saw the Popes' vestments reflected in the costumes of Elvis, Freddie Mercury, James Brown, Mick Jagger, and the WWF.

Legends of saints and the holy family were ingrained in us at an early age. We were bombarded with religious books and the famous, *Catholic Catechism*. Techniques ranged from benevolent compassion, to brainwashing and fear. Hell was made real and no Italian wanted to go there.

The most fearful ritual of Catholicism for me was confession. My mother made my brother and me confess to the parish priest once a month. Some priests would only listen and assign prayers for penance, but others would interrogate you. We had to complete a self-examination of our conscience to know our sins before we went into the confessional. As a youngster, I would go to confess and it would be something like this:

I would enter the confessional, and the priest would slide back a small window. A shade would be over the window so I could only see a silhouette of the priest.

The confession would begin; "Bless me, Father, for I have

sinned." Then I would proceed to tell him of my sins. Since I was so young, my sins would consist of, "I disobeyed my mother three times." (She was very forgiving.) "I disobeyed my father once." (He beat the hell out of me.) "I looked at a *Playboy Magazine*." (Sinful but fun) "I have thoughts about my classmate Laura." (I thought he might respond that he had heard the rumors.) "I use profanity every time the St. Louis Cardinals lose." (I still do that today but only in key games. I have matured.) To acknowledge the conclusion, I would say, "Please forgive me of these sins and the sins of my past." The priest would absolve me of my sins and assign penance, such as "Say five Hail Marys and five Our Fathers."

After confession one Saturday, I was walking home and a pretty girl named Sherry was standing in her front yard. She called for me to come over by saying, "My mother and father are not home, and I'm scared. Will you stay with me until they return?" All of a sudden I was scared. What did this girl want me to do? Was I going to have to return to confession? She continued, "Do you want to go inside and wait?" She was sending signals like a traffic light, stuck on green.

Her house was only one block from the elementary school's dark, vacant auditorium made famous by Laura. No Mrs. Butler to save me from sin this time. At that moment, I received some love from above. Sherry's mother and father arrived just in time to save their daughter from the clutches of an adolescent social lightweight. They also saved me from some life-threatening embarrassment. As I walked off, I winked at Sherry indicating, you don't know what you missed. Neither did I.

I invented games in church to survive a long mass or a priest that I didn't like. Some Sundays, I had to play these games or I would nod off like a Catholic narcoleptic. One game was church baseball. I would pick two baseball teams--always my beloved St. Louis Cardinals and some opponent.

These were the rules of the game:

1. One out per inning
2. Open the prayer book, Missal, or Hymnal
3. The last number on the page represents the action on the field

4. If the page ended with a "one" that was a single, "two" was a double, "three" was a triple, and "four" was a home run. Five, six, seven, eight, nine and zero were outs.

I would broadcast the game to myself in my mind. "Up for the Cardinals is third baseman Kenny Boyer. Here's the pitch (open the book page 42); there's a hard hit ball in the left center field gap. Boyer rounds first, heading for second. Here comes the throw from Mays, SAFE!" I could even simulate crowd noise by breathing deep into two hands over my mouth. Not only did I use this technique to get through Sunday High Mass, I have used it in waiting rooms, faculty meetings, college classrooms, and on long trips. What a tool for the mind or am I just a tool for doing it?

Another game I imagined was modernizing the Catholic Church. Today, what I admire and treasure most is the history and traditions of Catholicism. However, as a restless boy in church, these thoughts passed through my mind. Bless me father if I have sinned.

1. Monsignors and the Pope could add a propeller to their beanies.
2. Communion hosts should be different colors that reflect a corresponding fruit flavor.
3. Good looking nuns should have a different wardrobe than the others.
4. The priest could walk down the aisles of church shooting holy water blessings from a squirt gun.
5. Hide a secret microphone and camera in the confessional. (Remember Candid Camera)
6. A priest's sermon should consist of questions, after which the priest would give away prizes for correct responses like a game show. (Catholic Jeopardy with your host Father Patrick.)
7. Sell lottery tickets to win the tithe collection at the end of mass. Italians like gambling. Mass attendance would probably be higher, and the collections would be worth the gamble.
8. The priest could perform magic tricks and try to pass them off as miracles.
9. The priest could moonwalk across the altar during the service.

10. Parishioners could roast marshmallows over votive candles.
11. Make Juju beads rosaries. After every Hail Mary, eat one of the beads to better keep up with your prayers.

I give my permission to the Ecumenical Council of the Vatican to adopt any of these changes.

There were other mind games like rate the girls, rate the girls' mothers, the ugliest parishioner at the mass, pick a pew and bet on who would not be receiving communion, predict the length of the sermon, or man, woman, boy or girl who would walk in next. Then there was "I Dare You to Do This":

1. Leave a *Playboy* magazine in the pew with a prominent parishioner's name on it.
2. Walk up to the altar, grab a candle and light a big cigar.
3. Take out a straw and blow bubbles in the holy water font.
4. Make out with a girl in a vacant confessional booth.
5. Take twenty dollars in change from the collection basket before dropping in your twenty.
6. Take Jesus down from the cross.
7. Put an orange wedge and cocktail umbrella in the priest's wine chalice.
8. Talk to the priest before mass and attach a "kick me" sign to the back of his robe.
9. Release a mouse on the floor during a crowded mass.

Young Catholics are taught that if you have a serious problem, discuss it with a priest. I followed this advice only once. I made an appointment with the priest of another church so I wouldn't be recognized. He told me to meet him in the church after school. I waited in a pew near the front when I heard the cathedral door open. Walking slowly down the aisle was a very old priest who might retire before he reached me. I was about to be counseled about a girl problem from a seventy-six year old priest who had never had a girlfriend, but his goodness came through, and his message was about respect for yourself and respect for others. He advocated prayer and said my prayers would be answered according to God's will. He blessed me and left the cathedral. I lit a votive candle and said my prayers. For good measure, I carved a heart in the pew with mine and my girlfriend's initials so God could see how serious I was.

The Catholic religion sustains me today. My regret is that I sometimes strayed from what I was taught and who I should be. Looking back at my indiscretions, I now realize I did not have the spiritual maturity to overcome some temptations. I tried to swim in the deep end of life without a lifeguard or vest. I pray each day that I will be forgiven and have the strength to confront problems and temptations in the way of Jesus Christ. My personal exorcism continues today. All things have a defense mechanism. Bees can sting, spiders bite, opossums play dead, and skunks and big Italian women spray a foul odor. My defense mechanism was my religion. I continue to thank Jesus for saving my ass so many times.

19. What Bible passage is: "*If God is for us, who can be against us?*"
   A) Romans 8:31
   B) John 3:16
   C) Matthew 17:20

Part One

Answers 1-19

1. Where was the immigration processing center for Europeans in New York?

   B) Ellis Island

   Seeking a better way of life, immigrants came to America in large numbers from Europe during the years 1870-1900.

2. What is the original definition of a ghetto?

   B) An ethnic neighborhood

   Ethnic groups from Europe settled in the same areas of the large northeast cities. This provided for a common culture that made them feel more secure.

3. Who was chosen as the most famous Italian-American of the twentieth century?

   A) Al Capone

   Al Capone is the Italian most people have heard about. Crime made his a recognizable name. Italians will always be identified with crime. It is part of history.

4. What television family of the 1950s was truly a real-life family?

   C) The Nelson family of *The Adventures of Ozzie and Harriet*.

   They epitomized the family values of the 1950s. Their son Ricky became a teen idol and was best known for his singing career.

5. What figure appeared in early television test patterns?

   B) Indian Chief

   The test pattern was used for black and white sets only. It served the specific purpose of adjusting the black, white and gray colors on the screen. The test pattern and the Indian Chief became cultural icons of early television.

6. Who co-starred with Annette Funicello in the "Beach" movies of the 1960s?
A) Frankie Avalon
After Annette moved on from the *Mickey Mouse Club*, she became a teen idol and starred with Frankie Avalon in a series of "Beach" movies. Singer and song-writer, Paul Anka wrote his hit song, *Puppy Love*, about Annette, whom he was dating at the time.

7. What city was the location of the broadcast of *American Bandstand*?
C) Philadelphia
The building that hosted *American Bandstand* was located at 46th Street and Market Street in West Philadelphia. The African-American version of the show was *Soul Train.*

8. Where did Dr. Christiaan Barnard perform the first human heart transplant in 1967?
A) Cape Town, South Africa
Dr. Barnard performed the first human heart transplant on December 3, 1967. The surgery lasted nine hours and was assisted by a team of thirty medical workers. The patient, 54-year old Louis Washkansky, survived for eighteen days.

9. What was the first African-American television show?
C) Amos'n Andy
Amos 'n Andy was a comedy show that began in 1951. The cast were all African-Americans with the lead role played by Tim Moore. African-Americans were critical of the show because of the speech patterns and shadiness of the characters.

10. When Elvis first appeared on the *Ed Sullivan Show*, what stipulation was made by the host Ed Sullivan?
C) Television cameras could only show Elvis from the waist up. At first, Sullivan refused to invite Presley on, insisting that rock and roll music was not fit for a family show. Elvis would move his hips in suggestive ways. Parents condemned rock and roll music.

11. Who was the first African-American singer to be given his own musical television show?
    A) Nat King Cole
    In 1956, NBC gave Nat King Cole his own fifteen-minute musical variety show. In 1958 after sixty-four episodes, NBC cancelled the show after failing to secure a national sponsor.

12. What original member of *The Beatles* was replaced by Ringo Starr?
    B) Pete Best
    He had been with them since their early days and was part of the group for more than two years. At a recording session, a supervisor suggested using a different drummer.

13. Who did *Rolling Stone Magazine*, list as the number one singer of all time?
    A) Aretha Franklin
    Their top ten was 1) Aretha Franklin 2) Ray Charles 3) Elvis Presley 4) Sam Cooke 5) John Lennon 6) Marvin Gaye 7) Bob Dylan 8) Otis Redding 9) Stevie Wonder 10) James Brown

14. Who released a song and album in 1977 titled *Cat Scratch Fever*?
    C) Ted Nugent
    The song is about a man's long history of promiscuous sex. The title refers to the sexually transmitted disease syphilis. "Cat scratch fever" was a common slang term for the disease.

15. What was a slang term for a speakeasy during the Prohibition Era?
    C) A Blind Tiger
    Patrons bought bootleg liquor but did not look or seek to find out who sold it. They were blind to the illegal process to protect the bootlegger. The term "speakeasy" meant that people did not speak of such places on the streets.

16. What amendment eventually repealed the 18th Amendment?
    C) 21st Amendment
    Prohibition became too difficult to control. Federal agents were being killed trying to enforce the law and gang violence escalated.

17. What crime was Al Capone convicted of and imprisoned for in 1931?
    B) Income tax evasion
    Even though he was suspected of murder, extortion, and bootlegging, Al Capone was only found guilty of tax evasion. While in prison, Capone had no regard for the prison social order. An amusing story about Capone in prison was when he tried to cut in line to get a haircut, an inmate grabbed a pair of scissors and held them to Capone's throat. Capone said, "Do you know who I am?" The inmate retorted, "If you don't get back in line, I'll know who you were."

18. Who won the Academy Award for Best Actor in the 1972 film *The Godfather*?
    A) Marlon Brando
    Marlon Brando boycotted the ceremony, sending American-Indian Rights activist Sacheen Littlefeather to state his reason, which was his objection to the Hollywood depiction of American-Indians. Al Pacino also boycotted the event because he was insulted at being nominated for Best Supporting Actor rather than Best Actor.

19. What Bible passage states, "*If God be for us, who can be against us?*"
    A) Romans 8:31
    I like the odds.

Part Two

School Days and Nights

Chapter 10

Descending the Social Ladder

In junior high school, I had acquired some validation because I made the football team. It was unusual for a younger player to make the team. We had a great team and lost only one game. The older players were great athletes and a year or two older than their grade in school. One player even drove a car to school.

An unforgettable memory was leaving practice one day as the star player got into his car. He had some of his friends with him, and they stopped to offer another boy a ride, or so I thought. As the conversation escalated, they pulled him head first into the front seat and drove away with his legs dangling out the front passenger window. Fists were flying from the passengers in the front and back seats. The car stopped abruptly, they pushed the dangling boy out, and he ran away. I learned never to ride with strangers, team mates or even friends, at this school.

I did my best to please my teachers, but once I was removed from class for being a disruption, though I honestly didn't know why. We were having a lesson in grammar, and the English teacher wrote on the chalkboard, "There are no hills in Louisiana." Then she asked me what was "in Louisiana?" I did not know she was asking for the part of speech, so I answered, "No hills." The class erupted with laughter. I seriously thought that was the response she wanted. There it was, written on the chalkboard.

She chastised me for my conduct and not taking education seriously. Then she said, "I'm going to ask you one more time. What is "in Louisiana?" More befuddled at what was taking place, I paused and again said, "No hills." She quickly opened her desk drawer and proceeded to write a referral about my conduct and my lack of respect. Off to the discipline office I went for simply being myself.

Another episode with the same teacher bears repeating. We were reading a story about India and how the Hindu people used cow dung for fuel. Believe me, I didn't know what "dung" was, so I asked, "Mrs. Blair, what is cow dung?" Again, she thought I was being disruptive and uncaring, and away I went. Couldn't she give me some credit for being dumb? I knew "dung" by another four letter word. I felt like dung as I exited the class. Since then, I have become more educated. And that's no feces, manure, poop, crap, guano, waste or dung.

I had a math teacher named Mr. Bray, whom everyone liked, including me. He was a good teacher. When he would check roll at the beginning of class, rather than call me by my name, he would refer to me as the "Irishman." I assumed he was making fun of my Italian name. I smiled, the class laughed, and I thought that was the end of it. However, since he had gotten a laugh the first time, he began calling me "Irishman" every day, though I began to ignore him.

When he continued to call me 'Irishman," I would not answer because that was not my name. Somehow, he was offended by my lack of respect. He was really beginning to piss me off. He could make the class laugh at my expense. It was my turn to make the class laugh.

During the next class he referred to me as "Irishman" again. I did not answer. He said I was being disrespectful. He offered, "Irishman, if you don't like it in here, you need to get out." I got up and said, "Sure, Mr. Dickhead." The boys laughed and the girls were traumatized. So I miscalculated a little.

The assistant principal in charge of discipline called my mother and told her how disrespectful I had been to Mr. Bray. I had to apologize to him to get back in class. After that, he stopped calling me Irishman and I stopped calling him Mr. Dickhead. Well, not to where he could hear me.

I had earnestly tried to improve, or better yet, begin a social life. The "name" girls were pretty members of the honor society, cheerleaders, student council, class reporters, and teachers' pets destined for fame. They were definitely not interested in me. Stated another way, they were members of "Who's Who," and I was a member of "Who?"

Once upon a time very long ago
Marilyn was my Rapunzel princess and I was her beau
Her beauty and charm remain with me
In a delightful memory
Johnny-Giovanni

With my struggles in class and ethnic look, I was relegated again to the "other" category, but then along came Marilyn. My first real school girlfriend, a beauty that was overlooked because she was not a member of the campus ego club. We talked, we listened to music, we held hands, and she didn't reject my amateur kisses. Her heart was my home, and I wanted to love, honor, obey, and a lot of other things. At school, she wore my jacket, and I wore a smile on my face, a song in my heart, and a wish in my pants.

One Saturday, we went downtown to see the movie *G.I. Blues*, starring Elvis Presley. Infatuated with each other while sitting in the dark theater, we watched the movie three consecutive times. Elvis finished second that day, thank you very much.

On another occasion, her mother took us to an out of town football game. The ride home was a journey of delight. Marilyn and I cuddled under a blanket in the back seat. When we covered ourselves with the blanket, I was welcomed to Fantasy Island. You could feel the eleckissity! It was a two-hour fantasy ride home to a destination that I did not want to reach. For you deviant thinkers, nothing was lost in the back seat that night except some loose change. When we did arrive home, I was high on happy.

My best junior high school memories are of Marilyn, but my stupidity led us apart. I so loved her long auburn tresses, a perfect match for her complexion and makeup. Her beauty was imprinted in my mind when we were apart. One weekend she changed to a shorter, more stylish look, and I sulked over the loss of those beautiful slender strands of delight. Unhappy with my reaction to her new look, Marilyn found someone who appreciated the new style. I wish I could have a do over.

Thanks, Marilyn for being a great girlfriend, my dream lover, and the first entry on my cherished Mt. Rushmore of girlfriends.

Here is my dance and it goes like this
The name of the dance is the Rigor Mortis
Johnny-Giovanni

In the seventh grade, I was invited to my first girl-boy social birthday party. It was going to be at night in the backyard of a pretty neighbor's house. The possibilities of delight were endless in my mind. I was invited to a nighttime party with girls. I was Bill Clinton-happy!

I wanted to make a good impression so I could be invited to another nighttime birthday party. People were dancing, the party lights were dim, and I was dimmer. One of the pretty girls asked me to dance, not knowing that I had never danced with a girl before. Motionless, I held her hand with my left hand and put my right hand on her waist. I stood there for the length of the song, not moving and not saying a word. Today, there is a danced named after me. The Rigor Mortis.

As the party continued, a dance contest was held. It was the limbo so I felt better because no one had to have a dance partner. As I watched the dancers rhythmically swaying under the limbo stick to the beat of the music, I lost all confidence. As each dancer went under the limbo bar, everyone would applaud.

Totally psyched out, I knew it was my turn. I knew the applause would turn to laughter. I couldn't do the Rigor Mortis again. You had to have a partner. The party goers were looking at me, and I didn't know what to do. I panicked and raced toward the limbo bar and jumped over it. I got some unexpected applause. The jump was a ten, but the landing was a one. I fell and rolled across the yard, tearing a hole in the knee of my good pants, followed by the laughter that I feared.

The party was becoming a monumental disaster for my reputation. My worst decision was yet to take place. The birthday cake was German chocolate. I had never had German chocolate cake before, just mostly cannolis.

I looked at the frosting, and for some insane Italian-reason, I concluded that the coconut was chopped onions. I could even smell that they were onions. Being Italian, I had obviously seen more onions than coconuts. I was thinking how to politely refuse a piece of cake that had chocolate frosting with chopped onions.

As my place in line approached, I told the adult cutting the cake that I was going to pass. She insisted that I take a piece of cake and that I would like it. For some reason, my mind processed that as a threat. As she was speaking to me while holding the knife, she moved toward me. I thought I was being attacked. Instinctively, I grabbed the blade of the knife, and her reaction was to pull the knife back. As the knife retracted from my closed hand, I saw blood rise up through my clinched fingers, and I ran home. I don't know why I wasn't invited back the next year. I was the greatest show on earth. Since I had to leave in a hurry back then, I would now like to wish you a very belated "Happy Birthday, Sharon." Call me.

It was like a curse was following me around. I was born to be unpopular, and my science teacher must have known it. He was performing an experiment in class about the purification of water. He took a small glass of water from the classroom aquarium. The aquarium had plants, fish (some alive), turtles, rocks, and whatever the class threw in it when he was not looking. He boiled the glass of aquarium water and poured it over ice. He asked for a volunteer to drink it.

The students shrieked, made faces, held their noses, turned their heads, and some pretended to faint. When no one volunteered, he said, "I'll just call on one of you." It was the wrong time to become popular. Out of a class of twenty-eight he called on me. The one we can most do without if something goes wrong. Maybe he thought it wouldn't hurt an Italian because they probably have had worse. Not showing any sign of fear, I drank the glass of water. The class avoided me like I had a disease. "Don't touch him, he drinks sewer water!" "How do fish eyes taste?" "The creature from the Black Lagoon!" "Swamp breath!" The girls that didn't like me now disliked me even more. My legacy continued to grow.

There is an annual festival in our city called Holiday in Dixie. A parade was planned, and the committee asked the school for some students to ride on a float. The theme of the float was the United States Navy. It should have been *The Strange Island of Dr. Moreau* (a novel by H.G.Wells).

The float was constructed to be an aircraft carrier. My science class was my home room class, and each homeroom teacher was to select a student to ride on the float in the parade. Mr. Perkins chose me. Was he trying to make up for the water purification experiment that had driven away my classmates?

I asked around school to find out who else was going to be on the float. I couldn't find any information on who my fellow sailors would be. We were to wear blue jeans, a white tee shirt, and a sailor cap they gave us. As I arrived at the float, my fellow seamen were a collection of misfits, rejects, mutants, and losers from school. Now I knew why Mr. Perkins selected me.

I tried to go AWOL before the parade, but I got caught. I was forced to get on the float. As we navigated the parade route, I tried to hide my face, but my classmates in attendance would point at me and laugh. Too bad our ship was not equipped with machine guns, or I would have fired into the crowd. I felt like going overboard, but the sea below was the concrete pavement of the street. I rode out the imaginary waves and remained part of the lame gang.

Chapter 11
Finding Camelot

Just as Dick Clark dropped the traditional New Year's ball in Manhattan on January 1, 1961, I felt like the ball had dropped on me. The unpaved street I lived on in the city was subjected to numerous changes in school zoning. It seemed each new school year my residence would be assigned to a different high school. Didn't anybody want us?

The 1961 zoning change was exactly what I didn't need. I was zoned into the flagship school of the district. It was considered the best public school in terms of academics, athletics, and alumni. With its rich tradition of success and influential graduates, it also hosted an upper class clientele from which I was far removed. Many of the city's civic and business leaders were alumni of the school, and their families had traditionally followed their success through those hallowed halls of academia.

Inside the school was a Hall of Fame featuring pictures of many of the successful graduates. There was a United States Senator, city mayors, industrial and business leaders, medical professionals, military officers, writers, entertainers, and athletes. None of the inductees had last names that ended in a vowel. The Italian era had not reached the school yet, but I was going to change that. After my barely average junior high school career, I was ready to succeed or over-achieve. "You want me on that wall. You need me on that wall." So I thought.

I stepped off the city bus and headed toward the high school. Strangely, no one was following me. I was the only student taking public transportation to school that day. I was at the best school in the city, and many people still believe that today. To my surprise, there was no confetti parade for me …yet.

As I walked around, I did not see a familiar face. Most of my friends went to the new public high school near our old junior high. My insecurities began to surface, so I stayed alone. I wanted to fit in, but I felt as if I didn't belong. It was more my fault than the other students'. At lunch, I spotted one of the football coaches. Hoping he had some knowledge of who I was, I introduced myself. I briefly told him of my athletic background and asked if I could try out for the football team. He asked, 'What junior high school did you attend?" I told him, and then he said, "We don't have any more uniforms." Athletics was my calling card, and I had just been trumped.

What he said may have been true, but to an introverted wanderer seeking any kind of approval in an unfamiliar environment, it was catastrophic. What was I to do? For the remainder of the day, I could not concentrate in class. All I felt since I arrived was rejection. How was I going to survive at this school? How was I going to make friends?

As I walked to the bus stop that afternoon, I knew I never wanted to go back to that school. In the eighth grade, I was given an opportunity to go to the Catholic private school, but I had turned it down. It was an all boys' school, and they were required to wear uniforms, and a blazer and tie on some days. I had heard about how difficult the curriculum was, and how students also went to church every Wednesday. Those things scared me away, and on top of all that, the instructors were priests and nuns. Today, it is still one of the top private schools in the area. I made a mistake by not going.

Nevertheless, when I returned home that afternoon, I was speechless and had no appetite. The first thing my mother said was 'How was school today?" After a lengthy pause, I force out a reply, "Fine." I had already decided that I was never going back, and I had a plan: catch the bus, pretend to go to school, hang around somewhere all day, catch the bus, and return home.

This plan worked well for a while until some teacher decided to do her job and called my house checking on my absences. Making my mother promise not to tell my father, I explained my version of the events to her. She took me to the school board office the next day to apply for a transfer to the new high school where my friends attended. It would be the beginning of three of the best years of my life.

John F. Kennedy won the presidential election of 1960 to usher in the "New Frontier." Tragically, he was assassinated before the completion of his term. After his death, an article was written on his presidency, describing it as Camelot, a magical moment in history.

As JFK had his Camelot, so did I. Camelot was the castle of the legendary King Arthur with its adventures and romances. My Camelot was Woodlawn High School with its adventures and romances. Our mascot was the "Knights," and our school was referred to as the castle. Was this a coincidence? No way! Destiny was on our side and still thrives in each of us today. I love WHS! It is my only surviving love from high school.

The male students were gallant knights, and the female students were as beautiful and elegant as the fair ladies of Camelot. It was as idealistic as could be. There was neither a student nor teacher that I didn't like. Woodlawn was a collection of talented students from good homes and exceptional character that could match or best any school in the area. We all supported each other in forging a lasting tradition that we are all still proud of today. I loved my classmates and think of them often.

Jack, Mitch and me
52, 74, and 33
Always together, always alone
Johnny-Giovanni

One that has passed on was my best friend, Jack. Like me, Jack had very little to offer but was willing to share it with anyone. He was somewhat misunderstood by others because of his eccentric ways. There was a hidden effort in everything he did that few people knew. Jack was a relentless football player at practice and in a game. Any time we were playing pickup basketball, tennis, or were just working out, his effort would exceed all others.

One day, Jack and I decided to play a round of golf. We knew nothing about golf, and of course, had never played before. We rented some clubs and shoes from the clubhouse. We bought some golf balls (the cheapest ones but not near enough) and started on our adventure. From the beginning, it was embarrassing. We didn't anticipate that other groups of golfers would be playing behind us. Since I played baseball, I didn't think golf would be much different. On the first tee, I swung and missed twice before making contact with the ball that went out of bounds, and I could not find it. How much was this going to cost? One stroke and one lost ball. Jack wasn't much better, and we were to do this for 18 holes with people watching.

Jack and I got together and changed the rules to benefit our game. The first rule we instated was you could either hit the ball or throw the ball, but you must alternate. So, our tee shots began to be how far we could throw the ball, and we could easily find where it landed. On the second shot, we would use one of the clubs, any one of the clubs. Once we got on the green, we had to putt because that was fun.

By the 18th hole, the sun had gone down, the course was vacant, we bought balls three times, our throwing arms were sore, and we had lost two clubs. To acknowledge our effort, we both urinated in the 18th hole. That was our feelings about the game of golf. Our last rule was if anyone suggested playing golf again we would slap some sense into them.

Another great friend that has also passed on was Mitch. Mitch was big, strong, fast and athletic, and a menace to the opposition on the gridiron. Off the field, he was a gentle recluse lacking in confidence and seeking his first date with a girl. He had a slight speech impediment and rarely spoke. Living a great distance from the school, he walked back and forth twice a day to preseason football practice because he was too shy to ask for a ride.

I don't know if Mitch ever got a driver's license. The only date I remember him having was when one of my girlfriends fixed him up with her sister. Her sister was still in junior high school, and Mitch was a senior. We didn't tell Mitch how young she was, not that it would have mattered to him. We went to the lovely ladies' house that night and just visited. After the visit on the drive home, Mitch's speech impediment was worse. It was like he was stuttering a foreign language, yet he had a smile on his face like the full moon that night. I'm forever appreciative to those two sweet young ladies for making my friend happy. Mitch would bring that one date up almost every time we talked. No one has ever gotten more out of one date than Mitch. I wish I could convey to all of our classmates how good and gentle of a person Mitch was.

Jack, Mitch, and I were as loyal as the Three Musketeers and sometimes as dim-witted as the Three Stooges. We had a fishing trip planned one Saturday. I drove to a small man-made lake at the power plant where my brother worked. We were not having any luck fishing. One of the power plant workers gave us a unique fishing tip. The banks of the lake were granite rocks. He told us to get in the water along the bank and reach into the rocks because fish often would hide there. Should we believe this guy?

Of course, Jack was the first to say he would try it. To our awe, he threw a fish on shore and then another. Mitch and I went quickly into the water to try our technique of catching fish with our hands. One thing bass master fisherman didn't tell us was there could be other things in the rocks as well. Mitch reached into the rocks-- fish, another fish, and then a small snake. Jesus-like, the three of us ran across the water, crawled, and rolled across those granite rocks for safety. It was just like in *The Bible*. Scratched, bleeding, and howling with laughter, we threw the fish back in the lake, then killed the snake a multitude of times. Jack said, "Do y'all want to go camping tonight?" At that point, Mitch and I threw him in the lake.

In addition to Jack and Mitch, there was Don, a handsome, strong, over-confident, sometimes nuisance who thought he could sway any girl. His pickup lines, though not always clichés, were often worse than clichés.

Don was bragging to me about a private school girl that he had met. She was having an early spring party for her classmates at her house, and Don wanted to go but wasn't invited. Though not invited, Don and I proceed to the party in an upscale part of town. There were many pricey cars parked near the house: two Mustangs, a GTO, a Lincoln Continental (no doubt Daddy's car), and some other costly models. There was no room for my 1953 green and rust Plymouth Cambridge, so I parked a couple of blocks away.

As we approached the party, we could hear music, talking, and laughter in a privacy-fenced backyard. We walked in, and Don saw the girl that he had met. The first indication of a possible problem was when she said, "What are you doing here?" That cutting remark didn't faze

Don. He made himself welcome and began to talk to the other girls. To Don's delight, it was a girl's only party. (She attended an all-girls school)

I tagged along but was canvassing the scene for an escape route for when her father would realize we were there. Then without knowing, Don began to make a spectacle of himself with lame remarks that were humorous only to Don. He was talking to a pretty young girl who was sitting at one of the party tables. She was taken in by Don's good looks. She patted the chair next to where she was sitting and said, "Why don't you join me?" Life of the party Don said, "It looks like somebody already put you together, and I must say they did a fine job." Don was not deterred by the silence.

His confidence was growing as fast as my embarrassment. Speaking with another girl, he said, "Now I know where I've seen you before, in my dreams." And the misses just kept on coming. The final absurdity was when Don asked another girl, "Excuse me, can you follow directions?" Confused, the youthful beauty answered, "Of course!" Don said slowly, "Then show me your room."

I left the party and waited across the street for Don. After a while, he came out the front door with the girl he knew. I waved to him that I was across the street. They kissed passionately, and as he crossed the street, she yelled, "Call me soon," and he said, "Okay." She walked back toward the party, and Don crossed the street where I was standing. He turned and yelled, "HEY, DEBBIE, is this soon enough?"

In my first encounter with Don, I did not know him very well. Jack and I were going to shoot pool on Saturday night and we were talking about it at school. Don invited himself to go along with us. We played pool until after midnight, and I was taking Don home. Jack was in the front passenger seat and Don in the back. Many houses at that time had a gas light in the front yard. Don told us that if you smashed the gas light, a ball of fire would erupt. I stopped the car in front of Don's house. He got out of the car and said, "Watch this." He walked to his next door neighbor's house and smashed their gas light with a brick from the flower bed. He waved good-bye and went into his house.

On weekends when we didn't have much money, we would go to the neighborhood bowling alley. We would meet at Jack's house and walk the three blocks to the lanes. We didn't go to bowl; we went to play pranks on the bowlers and to cheat the pinball machine.

Inside were tables and chairs, a grill, a pool table, a nursery and four pinball machines on the back wall. We sat at the tables and tried to think of ways to disrupt someone's night. A minor prank was filling the finger holes of the house bowling balls with various items. We started with the complimentary condiments from the grill: mustard, mayonnaise, and ketchup. We would sit near the ball rack and watch as the potential bowlers tried to find a bowling ball that fit their hand. Then, surprise! We would laugh at the reactions and obscenities of the unsuspecting bowlers. We even added to our arsenal of disgust by filling the balls with urine, ink, and my favorite, upside down thumb tacks.

The challenge of the pinball machine was to win illegally. Our best method was to pick up the back support legs of the machine and place our wallets under it to make the playing surface level. We would rack up enormous scores and free games. Young pinball players were amazed at our ingenuity. We were role models.

When we did bowl, the game was modified. Each bowler would put a dollar in the pot. The rules were as follows:

1. In the first frame you had to bowl opposite your dominant hand.
2. In the second frame the ball had to be delivered granny-style between the legs.
3. The third frame required a backwards roll of the between the legs,
4. The fourth frame was completed with your eyes shut. This was the blind man's frame.
5. In the fifth frame you could use your natural delivery, but everyone could distract you with derogatory and obscene remarks.

We would repeat the rules for frames 6-10. The highest score wins the money. It was a fun night of "bowling."

Every October, the state fair would come to our city, bringing carnival rides operated by men with hidden liquor bottles and less education than we had, over-priced food that barely passed inspection by the USDA and was more hazardous to your health than radioactive waste, and rigged games that insured you would lose. We flocked there to ride, eat, and try our luck.

All the guys often went in a group because we could not afford to take a date unless she wanted to jump the fence to avoid the admission price and pay her own way after that. Our entourage included Don, Jack, Mitch, and me. Don's purpose was to help us get lucky with the girls. It never happened. Jack was to analyze the environment and seek out the places where we would have the best chance at success. Mitch provided security. Remember Odd Job in the James Bond movie *Goldfinger*? Mitch was a much larger and a much stronger version of Odd Job. Mitch didn't need a steel-brimmed hat for a weapon. Odd Job would have no

Don

Jack

Mitch

Me

chance against Mitch. Why was I there? I didn't have any homework. Ever.

We would always wear our letterman's jackets and so would rivals from other schools. One night, we saw some football players from another school. They had dates, and we stared at each other as we passed by. We pointed and laughed trying to make it seem that it was cooler not to have a date.

Jack noticed the girls were each carrying a small teddy bear, the consolation prize they gave you when you didn't win. It made them look like losers. As we walked pass them, Jack had a great idea that only he could imagine. We saw a family that had won a large prize, the kind that is the envy of all fair goers. Jack convinced the father to let us rent the large prize for a few minutes so we could double back and walk past our foes and their girlfriends with the grand prize teddy bear. The man laughed and refused our money but agreed to let us hold the teddy bear.

We made our way back holding the big bear as our competition walked by. The girls were still grasping their small prize as we held up our "winnings." Don asked, "Would you girls like to walk around with some winners?" They didn't answer, and Mitch stuttered, "Th th that must mean yes."

For one last insult, Jack pretended he was giving our winning bear to the little girl who had loaned it to us. We didn't want to be seen "bearless" later on without a good reason. Jack was a genius, all of this right before the eyes of our nemeses and their girlfriends. They thought we had won the big prize and were charitable enough to care for a small child. It was all a lie. My friends were the best. My friends were the worst.

Mitch wanted to play one of the State Fair games. A basket was tilted at a 45-degree angle, and you had to lob a ball into the basket. If the ball stayed in the basket, you would win a prize. The sign read, "One ball for 25 cents or three balls for 50 cents."

Mitch bought one ball for 25 cents, tossed it at the basket, and it bounced out. As he was walking away, the game attendant said, "Hey Lucky, come back. This time I'm going to give you two balls for 25 cents." Mitch looked at us for approval and Don said, "That's a great deal. Take it." Mitch missed twice more, and we walked away. You do the math, we couldn't.

The night was coming to an end. We made our way past the freak show and stopped to look at the people on stage. The barker would bring some of the "freaks" out and some pretty extras to try to lure in customers. We were admiring the bearded woman and trying to determine if the beard was real, or if she was a man. The vote was deadlocked at two and two. Jack and I said she was a man; Don and Mitch swore she was a real woman. Then Don got a little naughty and a lot embarrassing. He shouted to the barker, "Make her stand on her head so we can tell if she is a woman." The comment did draw some laughs from bystanders. As we walked away, I sarcastically said to Don, "You're so funny you must be kin to Don Rickles." And only as Don would say, "I might be. We have the same name."

Our most reliable friend was Thomas. He was our designated driver. Alcohol was not involved; he just had the car most likely not to break down. Thomas was raised perfectly by very caring parents who wanted the best for their son. His only flaw to us was that he was too honest. If we ever got into trouble, he would most likely tell the truth, so we couldn't trust him. It was always fun with Thomas because knowing his parents taught him right from wrong, we would always try to convince him that wrong was more fun. He would never give in.

We were driving around downtown one night and saw the marquee on a movie theater with the letters, "XXX," and the title, *Not Tonight Henry*. We decided to take in the movie, a nudie film where a man named Henry chased around topless girls. Thomas wanted to leave, but Jack said no. Thomas claims he doesn't remember seeing the movie. We think he sat through the movie with his eyes closed because he was trained in good over evil. We could always depend on Thomas to do the right thing. He could always predict the failed outcome of our reckless behavior earning him the name "Nostrathomas." Of course, we didn't listen to him.

Chapter 12
The Dating Game

The 1960s didn't have online dating, but we did have inline dating, and my place was at the end of the line. All of those early experiences of humiliation, complete failure, and snide remarks by others had a negative influence on my self-esteem. My acceptance of their ridicule made me feel like my name didn't even deserve to have a capital letter.

Boys had to wait in line or have a significant achievement to have a chance to date one of the school beauties. Therefore, my thinking that I could date one of these amazing girls was asinine, or even worse, "asiten." Moreover, I had a fear of dating and not being successful. I didn't know jack about Jill. If my classmates had known that information about me, it would have been a laugh fest for them and home school for me. Who do you date at home school, a stuffed animal? No, that would be incest. I had a lot of doubt about myself, and before any date, I wondered how life would have been at the all boys' Catholic school that I should have attended.

After a lot of praying, and a couple of junior varsity touchdowns, I was ready to try dating. I had a girl on my radar screen for a while. Shirley was very pretty, very smart, and very popular. I gave her a check mark in all of the right boxes. I was very apprehensive about asking her for a date. It would be more like begging for a date. I was expecting "no" as an answer. I just hoped it wouldn't be followed by a long laugh.

I called her on a Thursday night for a Saturday night date, and she accepted. Did she know I was the one that called? The plan was to pick Shirley up at 6:30 P.M. and drive to a movie theater downtown for the seven o'clock feature. After the movie, we would go by the "school" Dairy Queen. I wanted to be seen with this stunning damsel. I needed the exposure, she didn't.

This first date was so important that I practiced Saturday morning. This wasn't just a first date, it was a date with Shirley. Maybe I shouldn't have started with the top of the social order. Undetected, I drove to her house so I would be familiar with the route. I pretended to go to the door and practiced what I was going to say. I drove from her house to the downtown movie theater carrying on a conversation with the empty passenger seat all the way. I parallel parked near the theater, got out of the car, and opened the passenger door for my lovely date. I walked up to the ticket booth pretending to buy two tickets to see *Period of Adjustment*, starring Jim Hutton and Jane Fonda.

The movie was based on a play by Tennessee Williams about two married couples having differing marital problems. Shirley would probably understand the plot but not this rookie dater. My expertise was more in the realm of horror pictures and cartoons. After pretending to watch the movie, I then drove to the Dairy Queen, engaged in more conversation with my imaginary date. I was so prepared that I even clipped a cheat sheet of topics to the sun visor in case the conversation lagged. I had to give my very best effort in hopes of a possible second date with the lovely Shirley.

At home, I watched the clock as it neared my departure time. My mom lectured me on treating a girl with respect. She made me swear to a vow of virginity but I was always committed to thinking outside the bun. I had heard this many times from my Mother and Chuck Berry. "Johnny, be good." I didn't want to be disrespectful and not listen, but I wasn't even thinking of getting to first base. I just didn't want to strike out. This was Shirley! I would never disrespect her. All I was thinking about was could I keep up a meaningful conversation and how many "uhs" were too many in a sentence.

This was my FIRST ever drive-a-car date. I even thought about stealing a better car for Shirley and then returning it after the date. Things had to be perfect. What was mom thinking? Did she not trust me? Did she think I would forsake responsibility at a time like this? I didn't want to jeopardize my dating career after one date. The pressure was on.

Zero hour approached, and I was on my way. As I drove, I envisioned Mom at home praying the rosary that her little boy would not do anything to embarrass himself or the family. She had nothing to worry about and neither did Shirley.

On the drive to Shirley's house, I was a little nervous and consumed my entire night's supply of peppermint Life Savers. I parked the car and went to the door reeking of peppermint and an overdose of Aqua Velva. When she opened the door, she looked amazing (and still does today). There she was, my first real date. I was like a Neanderthal that had just discovered fire. I was elated and she was hot. I was not as talkative as I was on my imaginary practice date, but we still had fun.

We went to the movie and then to the Dairy Queen and saw some friends. The evening was a success. I took her home just before eleven. We sat in the car a few minutes and talked. I walked her to the front door and she gave me a polite kiss on the cheek, and I was on my way home. She was much more exhilarating than any touchdown I had scored.

Nighttime kisses on Shirley's porch
Warmed my Italian heart
In the winter of '62
Johnny-Giovanni

I dated Shirley for a few months. We shared a wonderful Christmas together. I still remember the gifts she gave me: a green sweater with suede green leather patches at the elbow, a gift certificate, and an album by comedian Vaughn Meader, entitled *The First Family,* a comedic impersonation of the Kennedy family in the White House.

Those were the most gifts I had ever received for Christmas from one person. That Christmas, Shirley gave much more than she received. She embodied the Christmas spirit of giving; she was a real Santa Claus. Baffled by her generosity, my greedy hands ripped open the gifts afraid that she might take them back. I guess you could say I embodied the spirit Santa Claws.

Shirley was always a boost for my fragile psyche. If I needed to see a friendly face at school, magically she would appear. Being around her provided me with the encouragement I was not receiving anywhere else. I want success and happiness for all of my friends, but most of all for Shirley. Time with her was always good. In my dating life, I thought of Shirley as beautiful, kind, considerate, loveable, intelligent and a perfect future bride for some blessed man. Regrettably, it didn't turn out to be me. Unregrettably, it did for her.

If anyone could turn a house into home, it would be Shirley. If the sun burns out and needs to be replaced, Shirley would be the perfect equivalent. With a halo of radiance, she always provided warmth, and energy. If need be, she could probably turn water into Bud Light. Shirley was my "man on the moon moment." She married one of our high school classmates, and I know they are very happy. They are the true Mr. and Mrs. WHS. As I reflect back on the best damsel dozen, Shirley was the Faberge'. She could solve my emotional riddle and make me feel as if I belonged. She never hurt my feelings. Shirley is the flawless second entry on my Mt. Rushmore.

In October of 1962, a grave political situation emerged. The Cuban Missile Crisis was a Cold War confrontation between the United States, the Soviet Union, and Cuba. Soviet leader Nikita Khrushchev, and Cuban leader, Fidel Castro, conspired to place nuclear missiles in Cuba less than one hundred miles from the United States. The missiles were detected by a United States spy plane. The countries were on the brink of a nuclear conflict. President Kennedy considered an attack on Cuba but decided on a naval blockade to prevent Soviet ships from delivering the missiles. The maneuver was called a military quarantine. The President demanded that all offensive weapons be dismantled and returned to the Soviet Union. There was little hope that Khrushchev would agree.

20. What United States U-2 pilot was shot down and captured by the Soviet Union for spying in 1960?
    A) Francis Gary Powers
    B) James Doolittle
    C) Paul Tibbets

At school, preparations were being made for evacuation and safety. Soviet ships were approaching the blockade. Some of my friends and classmates did not attend school that day in fear of a nuclear strike. I did my best to warn my mother of this dangerous situation and I asked to be allowed to stay home. She told me my father would be home, and I would be safer at school. She was right. Which would I rather face, the threat of Khrushchev's missiles, or my father's wrath? Off to school I went.

My English teacher was crying telling us she may never see her son again. There was alarm in the faces of many. Then the news came that the Soviet ships had turned back. Secret negotiations had ended the conflict and calm was restored.

After the Cuban Missile Crisis, President Kennedy's popularity increased, and so did mine. His was understandable, mine was not.

I need some help here. Sing it, Andy Williams. *Where do I begin?* There was a junior high cheerleader that I had noticed a year before. The school she attended played a football game at our high school's practice field. When I first saw her, I stood in frozen ecstasy. She was the most beautiful girl I had ever seen with her blonde hair, pretty face, perfect little nose, and a matching body. She was a masterpiece of creation born to beautify the world.

Continue, Andy. *With her first hello*, she caught me staring and flashed a smile that left me gasping for air. Who was this lovely image of perfection, this enchanting Aphrodite? I had to find out her name and where she would be attending high school.

Some of my teammates gave me the information I was seeking. Her name was Jan, and she would be attending WHS. That was the good news. The bad news was she also was well-acquainted with many boys from other schools, and it was easy to understand why. The competition was going to be insurmountable, but for a chance to date her, I was a willing to take an emotional beat down. This was only one of many to follow. I spent the rest of that school year and the entire summer waiting for her.

In the fall of '63
Leaves dangled and fell from the school yard tree
An apparition in my mind would swirl
While thinking about that beautiful girl
Johnny-Giovanni

As the new school year dawned, I scanned the campus for her debut. On that hot August day when I saw her again, my life got forever better and worse. It was a one-sided love story. Croon it again, Andy. *She gave new meaning to this empty world of mine.* She was campus royalty.

Watching her every move, I observed from a distance. I made mental notes of her friends, her classes, her lunch shift, the routes to her classrooms, and especially of the other boys that would be my competition. I subtly asked questions about her to gather as much information as I could.

When the reconnaissance phase was over, I was ready to take a chance even though I felt unworthy to be around her. She was walking to her class, and I had positioned myself by a locker so she would pass me. As she approached, I said, "Uh, Uh, Uh," and she walked past before I could collect myself. My plan was a good one, but I had forgotten to plan what I was going to say. After hours of thought, I came up with, "Hi, how do you like school so far?" I must have rehearsed that line a thousand times. I had to be at my best.

The next day, there I was again, waiting for my next attempt at humiliation. As I greeted her, I was surprised at how nice she was. She smiled and responded that she liked school. Her gentleness gave me the confidence to talk her. After a few days of meaningless conversation, she gave me her phone number and said I could call her sometime. I asked, "When is sometime?" She replied, "Tomorrow will be good."

That night I could not sleep. My inclination was to call then, but she said tomorrow. I looked at the clock and it was 11:54 P.M. In six more minutes it would be tomorrow. Continue my love story, Andy. *Can love be measured by the hours in a day?* Those six minutes seemed like dog minutes as I watched the clock. At one minute past midnight, I began dialing the number, and then suddenly stopped. That was not a good plan. My mind was a ball of confusion. This girl was making me feel good in a bad way.

When I saw her at school the next day, I told her I almost called her at 12:01 because technically that was the next day. She laughed and said I should have. Did I hear that right, **I should have!!** Then she invited me over to her house for Friday night. I was ecstatic. Spontaneously, I asked one of the most brainless questions ever, "Do you know I'm Italian?" She laughed, thinking I was trying to be funny. I could be funny by not saying anything. I was serious because one mother of the past didn't want her daughter to date an Italian. She told me I was fun to talk to, and she would see me Friday night.

Friday night arrived, and I went to her house. She looked amazing and smelled wonderful. We went into the living room and watched television. She had prepared a large bowl of popcorn that was on the coffee table. We talked, laughed, and watched television. You can have a great time with someone doing simple things, or was I just a simple person? Don't answer that.

As I was leaving, there was a little romance initiated by her at the door. It made the night more special. On the drive home, I could still smell the fragrance of her perfume and imagined the vision of her beauty. Jan was completely different than what I had expected. You cannot preordain what a girl is, not by her appearance, her color, her name, her religion, her occupation, her residence, her reputation, or even the rest of her family. Jan was beautiful, relaxed, confident, and much more experienced than I, but she never let it show. Jan became my number one squeeze.

How long does it last? You can stop there, Andy. Jan was always my date to major school functions. Having her by my side validated my place in the dating realm. Jan was always careful enough not to lead me on or to hurt my feelings. I never discussed it with her, but she knew that I wanted more of a relationship than she did. I don't know if it was immaturity or fear, but I accepted her terms.

Our final date that concluded our friendship was as fate had planned long before. My friends understood how much I cared for Jan. They were always questioning me about her and what we did when we were together. I know what they thought, but it was not true, and it was not going to happen. They also understood that I didn't have a chance with her. Our relationship was a lost cause. She had never mentioned her other dates to me, though I had heard about them. She was definitely a high school treasure that many others had found. For a short time, I was one of those others.

On a fateful Friday night, we shared our last date. We saw a movie and got something to eat at a drive-in. Upon arriving to her house, I could tell something was on her mind. She asked if we could talk in the car before I walked her to the door. Jan began crying, and I held her in my arms. She said what some people thought about her was hurtful and not true. She thanked me for always being respectful. I knew that my time with Jan had come to an end.

The dark, slow, painful, and final drive back home was like a funeral procession of one. I was driving the hearse that carried my lifeless dream. I never told her that I loved her, though I did. I was always aware that whatever this relationship could be labeled, it was going to end. Jan was like Halley's Comet streaking beautifully across my life. She was a brief, once in a lifetime, moment that I could not hold on to or comprehend. Her name and face are now forever in my mind. I think back to the first time I saw her, with her everlasting-smile. I think back to that first kiss, when I opened my eyes to see if it was really her. It is good that our time ended as it did so as to preserve the righteous innocence that it was. The time with Jan is one of the greatest moments of my life. She is the third monument on my Mt. Rushmore. Jan will always be the most beautiful girl in the history of WHS.

The next week, when I arrived at school, my friends wanted to know about my date with Jan. I told them, and of course, they all laughed. No one believed me. In their minds, there was much more to our date than the truth. They wanted the truth. They wouldn't believe the truth.

Although, my love story with Jan was only a week in the past, I was invited to a swim party by a young Italian beauty named Celeste. She attended the Catholic girls' school, and the date was a secret affair that I didn't want anyone to know about. Celeste's bosom was legendary among the boys at the local Catholic high school.

I really did not know Celeste and didn't care to, but attending a swimming party with her was worth a one-night investment. I arrived at her house and sounded the horn as she instructed. I didn't know why she didn't want me to come to the front door. Then it became obvious. She strategically stood in front of a shaded window. There they were. Two silhouettes on the shade. *Oh, what a lovely couple they made!* There was a pause then Celeste appeared. It was easy to see that the exit from her house was choreographed many times. I'm sure it worked every time, just as it did this time. If it was to make an impression, it did. I wanted this exit on film to watch over and over.

The drive to the party was going to be slow and rewarding. As she sat next to me in the car, I tried to look straight ahead, but my peripheral vision could see her ample assets. I tried to think wholesome thoughts, but my mind was not cooperating. When coming face to face with that bounty, I was a teenage male weakling. The imaginary devil on my left shoulder was saying, "Molest Celeste," while the mother figure on my right shoulder was preaching common decency and respect. To try and redirect my mind, I tried to think of the popes, priests and nuns, but they all wore an evil grin.

The parents of the girl hosting the party were in attendance keeping refreshments on the tables and chaperoning. Then they announced "game time." They rolled out two long soft rubber mats from the patio to the pool and placed a blow-up beach ball on each mat. The object of the game was that the girl member of each couple had to push the beach ball with her nose into the water and together with her teammate get the beach ball to the other end of the pool. The girls would start and the boys would be behind them.

Undoubtedly, the host's father must have thought of this game because there he was near the pool with his camera focused on Celeste. Of course, Celeste and I were in the first group. The girl next to us got down on all fours on her mat, prepared to push the beach ball. Celeste got down on all sixes, ready to move forward. The contest began, and Celeste made it into the pool first. With difficulty, she tried to swim. Yes, you evil thinkers, she was trying to do the breast stroke. It was obvious her breasts eclipsed her swimming talent, but no one cared.

I dove in behind her. My strategy was to swim past her underwater so she could throw me the ball and I would lead us to victory. While underwater, I paused to see where Celeste was. I could see that her bosom was about to escape from her swim suit. Her cupeth was definitely about to runneth over. I was mesmerized for a second and then remembered this was a swim contest. My competitive instincts took over and I swam hard passed Celeste and broke the water about fifteen feet in front of her. She passed me the ball, and as I headed toward victory, I was anticipating the celebratory hug that would be waiting. The only person happier than me at the finish line was the host's father filming the event. He was a dirty old man. I was a dirty young teen. Advantage, me.

At the party, I realized that Celeste was a risk-taking young lady. As we drove home from the party, we passed a business complex that had a lighted water fountain in the center of the parking lot. Celeste wanted to swim in the fountain. She got into the two feet deep water and lay down on her back. The lights in the fountain illuminated her body. She was amphibious; she looked great in the water, and on land. I admired the beautiful Celeste lying on her back in the shallow water surrounded by the lights. I named the vision "Two Coins in a Fountain." I wanted to pick up the change.

Part Two

Answer

20. What United States U-2 pilot was shot down and captured by the Soviet Union for spying in 1960?
A) Francis Gary Powers
Powers was shot down and captured on May 1, 1960. In February of 1962, he was exchanged for Soviet spy, Rudolf Abel. Powers was criticized for not destroying his aircraft and for not using his optional CIA issued suicide pill.

Part Three

The Sixties Scene

Chapter 13

Lovin' the Hippie Girls

The decade of the 1960s was tumultuous. People, countries, movies, and lifestyles demanded more freedom from the constraints of the previous society. There was war, civil rights issues, and violence. A cultural revolution, or "counterculture," was evolving, and the authorities, whether it be the government, parents, clergy, or the military, were being challenged with issues they were not prepared to handle. Being unprepared was status quo for me. Social scientists who study culture say it is part of the cultural cycle. Beliefs, morals, styles, families, and religions of the past were vanishing. Giovanni was more becoming Johnny. Did we really think we would live a generation and expect things to stay the same? *The Times, They are a-Changin'*, and so was I.

21. Who released the album *The Times, They are a-Changin'*?
    A) Bob Dylan
    B) John Lennon
    C) Joan Baez

When John F. Kennedy was elected president in 1960, there was much attention given to his election. One was the fact that he was Catholic. I was not, and am still not, a political person. I didn't care who won the election, but some people's belief was that we should never elect anyone from the Catholic faith.

22. Why were many people opposed to a Catholic president?
    A) People of southern European origin could not be trusted.
    B) They feared the president may have Mafia connections.
    C) If elected, his or her allegiance might be to the Pope.

As the greatest decade in history (the 1960s) moved on with its social revolution and counterculture, my moral foundation began to falter. The sights and changes were more than I could withstand. The hippies and flower children of the Sixties wore bell-bottoms, halter tops, had long hair, flashed the peace sign, displayed beads, headbands, fringe and my personal favorites, miniskirts and no bra. My curly unmanageable mane was now in style. They listened to rock music, took drugs, and had a free and independent lifestyle. I was falling in love with girls I didn't know over and over again. I loved the hippie girls and their carefree attitude. Until the hippie girls, the only female breast that I had ever seen was my Aunt Cella breast feeding my cousin Vincent, and it looked as if he didn't like it.

Here is a parody of some classic 1960s slang. The counter culture rejected *The Man*. They were what was *happening now*. They were *right on* with their *threads*. On weekends they would *hang loose* or *shack up* with their girl and would always try to avoid *the fuzz*. You could always have a date and a good time with *Mary Jane*. Your friends would not *fink you out* because they did not want to become a *candyass*. If you and your *chick* were *bummed out* because you were out of *bread*, you could always resort to *five-finger discount* or a trip to the *Midnight Auto Supply* to get some spare parts to sell. If you went back to your *pad* to *crash*, you had to be careful so your *old lady* wouldn't get *knocked up*. Maybe you could find another *hood* or two to *cut out* with, and the night could still be *far out man*. What does it mean?

The Man - those in charge, authority
happening now - what was important
right on - acceptable, agreement
threads - clothes, fashion
hang loose - relax and have a good time
shack up- stay overnight or live with a girl
the fuzz - the police
Mary Jane - marijuana
fink you out - report you, tell on you
candyass - wimp or snitch

chick - good looking girl
bummed out - disgusted with the situation
bread - money
five-finger discount - stealing, theft
Midnight Auto Supply - steal parts or items from other cars late at night
pad - house or apartment
crash - relax or sleep
old lady - your girlfriend
knocked up - get pregnant
hood - hoodlum or thug
cut out - leave, go somewhere
far out - a good time, amazing

23. One of the most popular hippie destinations of the Sixties was the Haight-Ashbury district. Where was it located?
    A) New York City
    B) Los Angeles
    C) San Francisco

24. What was the defining feature of hippies?
    A) They had only one name.
    B) They had long hair.
    C) They wore boots or sandals.

Possibly some of our young teachers at my new school were closet hippies. A peculiar and perplexing occurrence happened one day in my study hall class. It was a split class; half of the hour was before lunch, and the other half hour was after lunch. Mrs. Simpson was the teacher in charge. I guess she must have been in her late twenties, or early thirties.

The purpose of study hall was to do your homework, study, but above all else, keep quiet. I was whispering to Jack, and he said something humorous, and I began laughing. I tried to conceal the laughter, but I couldn't. Mrs. Simpson asked me to be quiet, but that just made the laughing more persistent. She said to me, "Come sit under my desk so you won't disturb the others." The space under a teacher's desk was about a three-foot cubicle enclosed on the front and sides and with an opening in the back where the teacher sat. As instructed, I placed myself in the cubicle to the laughter of the class. Then I noticed the crawl space became smaller and darker.

To my astonishment Mrs. Simpson's legs appeared facing me in the enclosed area. She was sitting at her desk in a tight skirt with her legs slightly separated. I was no longer alone. I had a view of what only Mr. Simpson should see. I could see the top seam of her stockings all the way up to her panties. I could even see her welcome mat. I did not want to move or touch her in any way. Was this done on purpose or did she have a lapse of judgment? The lunch bell rang, and the students in class left the room. Mrs. Simpson stood up and said, "Don't let this happen again." That assertion canceled my plans for after lunch, but study hall did become my favorite class. From then on, I tried to get in trouble.

I was friends with an older cute girl named Susan, who fiercely wanted to be a hippie. She was seeking acceptance and companionship, or possibly love, and would acquiesce in any way to achieve it. I liked Susan, but our style of living was too different to pursue anything other than a friendship. When Susan rented her first apartment, she gave me the address and told me I could come by anytime. On my way home one winter night, I decided to go visit Susan.

I knocked on the door, and a pretty girl opened the door. Not Susan. The apartment was very nice but dark with the glow of a single candle. Like Hotel California. *What a lovely place, what a lovely face.* I asked for Susan, and her roommate informed me Susan wasn't home but if I liked, I could come in and wait for her. *I was thinking to myself, this could be heaven or this could be hell.*

I entered the apartment to the smell of burning incense. I sat on a chair across from the couch. Susan's roommate chose the couch. I asked her name, and she answered Molly. Molly was dressed in a bath robe with a hood draping her shoulders and soft, brown suede leather boots. Molly looked good, making my thoughts bad. Was she wearing anything under that bath robe? Is " the devil made me do it" a legal defense? We talked normally for a while, but then the visit became strange.

Molly asked, "Would you like something to drink?" I answered with a soft, polite, "No." I was taken aback when she said, "I'll get it for you." Molly went into the kitchen and came back with a glass which appeared to have a clear type soda in it, possibly Sprite, and an empty cup. She handed me the empty cup and returned to sit on the couch. Bewildered, I didn't know what to do with the empty cup. Did she forget to fill it with a beverage, or was it just a plain cup of "No"? What would I say if she asked, "How do you like your "No"? Should I say, "Yes, I like No." What is an answer for being served an empty cup? Did she put something in my cup of No? How was I supposed to know when I finished my "No?" Was this some hippie mind game, was she on drugs, or was it just a simple mistake?

I decided to play along and check her reaction. I was like a kid at a four-year old's tea party pretending to drink something that wasn't in the cup. Getting anxious to leave, I asked Molly if she knew where Susan was. She put her legs up Indian-style under her butt and closed her eyes. I assumed she was trying to locate or communicate with Susan. After about a minute she opened her eyes and said, "Sorry, I can't find her."

My survival instincts said, "Don't act alarmed because it may offend her, and she could morph into something threatening." I thought things might return to normal when she asked, "Would you like to hear some music?" I answered the obligatory "Sure," and Molly started singing *Whiter Shade of Pale*, acapella, of course.

When she stopped singing, she asked, "What kind of girls do you like?" I knew a lot was riding on this answer, so I had to be extremely careful. I came back with, "Those that like me." I thought I had a checkmate, but she said, "I like you." I wanted to finish my cup of "No" and get the hell out of there. How would I know when I finished my "No?"

Trying to change the subject, I said, "Tell me something about yourself." Of all things, the girl said, "I only answer personal questions if they are asked in Spanish. I don't want anyone else to know about me." The only Spanish I had ever spoken was *"dos enchiladas* with *queso*." Fortunately for me, the telephone rang, and she went to answer it in the bedroom. While she was gone, I put down my cup of "No," careful not to spill a drop. *The last thing I remember, I was running for the door.* It was after midnight when I found my car, and I vanished into the night.

The hippie counterculture eventually declined but left us with some weird happenings, great music, fashion, and a colorful psychedelic chapter of the 1960s.

25. Which is a slang term for LSD?
    A) Acid
    B) Baby
    C) Silver Bullet

Chapter 14
Welcome to McDonald's

Another landmark that gained status in the 1960s was McDonald's. Operated by Richard and Maurice McDonald, it began as a barbeque restaurant in 1940. Businessman Ray Kroc joined the company as a franchise agent in 1955 and later purchased the company from the McDonald brothers. McDonald's filed for a U.S. trademark of the name "McDonald's" on May 4, 1961.

Millions have eaten from the McDonald's menu, received items from McDonald's promotions, and viewed numerous commercials and recited the jingles. However, there is one McDonald's commercial yet to be seen. I would imagine lying somewhere on a cutting room floor might be this:

A masked man holding a gun walks into a McDonald's restaurant.
McDonald's employee: "Welcome to McDonald's. May I take your order?"
Masked gunman: "This is a McHoldup. Give me all of your McMoney. McNow."
McDonald's employee: "Would you like a hot apple pie with that?"
Masked gunman: "McNo, just hurry the McUp."
McDonald's employee: "Let me see if I have that order correct. You want all of my McMoney and nothing else."
Masked gunman: "Okay, throw in a McNumber Two, and no McOnions. And McHurry!"
McDonald's employee: "Did you say a McFlurry?"
Masked gunman: "McHell no, just shut the McUp and get my McOrder McNow, you McMoron!!"
McDonald's employee: "Alright, all of my McMoney and a number two.That will be $5.48."
Masked gunman: "Here, you can keep the McChange."

McDonald's employee: "McThanks!"
Masked gunman: "You're McWelcome."
McDonald's employee: "Come Mc to see us."

26. The original McDonald's mascot was a man with a chef's hat on top of a hamburger-shaped head. What was his name?
 A) Donald
 B) Ronald
 C) Speedee

In the Sixties, McDonald's was a novelty, though today fast-food restaurants are everywhere. My friends and I would ride around and stop for some fast food at McDonald's. Once, I was driving around with a girl named Martha. I drove the car into a McDonald's parking lot; I went into the restaurant and picked up a couple of burgers, fries, and drinks while Martha remained in the car. I came back out and we sat in the car talked and ate our burgers and fries.

The French fries were served in a small paper holder. I finished my burger and was eating the French fries from the small paper holder when I decided to go back inside for another burger. Martha was wearing some hot little short shorts.

Holding my French fries, I got out of the car. I didn't want to go back into McDonald's eating French fries, so I leaned into the car window, tossed the fries to Martha through the window, and told her, "Keep these warm until I get back." She was unaware that I had thrown them until they landed right between her legs, resting next to her crotch on those small short shorts. Trying to be delightful, I said, "I just wanted you to keep them warm, not hot. Please let me get them." As I walked away from the car, the remaining fries whizzed over my shoulder and past my head. Another moniker for "fast food" at McDonald's.

Here are some little known specialties from the McMafia menu. This service is only available in "Little Italy" neighborhoods at McDonaldo's. You go to the drive thru window in your black four door sedan equipped with suicide doors and say, "Vito sent me." Then order one of the following:

1) Italian Big Mac -- Comes with secret instructions on the wrapper on how to contact Mafia hitman"Big Mac."
2) Italian McChicken -- Served only to those who fear the Mafia.
3) Italian McBroken Rib --Free with a coupon given to those who have been "worked over" by the Mob.
4) Italian Happy Meal -- Includes a small hamburger, small fries, and a secret fun time telephone number.
5) Italian "McSwimmin'with the Fish" -- Served as a last meal.
6) Italian McNuggets – You have solved the Jimmy Hoffa disappearance.
7) Italian Fifth Amendment Burger -- When the clerk asks, "May I take your order?" You answer, "I refuse to order on the grounds that it might incriminate me." The clerk will understand that you want a #7.
8) Body Bag Burger -- Packaged in an army green plastic wrapper labeled "CONTENTS DECEASED." This is a real collector's item.

Chapter 15

60's Classic Automobiles

In today's world, we are trying to conserve energy, but in the 1960s gasoline was plentiful. There was also a revolution in auto design. The Interstate Highway System was being constructed, and people wanted speed, power and eye appeal from their vehicles. To meet those needs, "muscle cars" entered the scene. Those cars were irresistible then and collector's items now, worth more than ten times their original value when properly restored. If you owned a muscle car, you had bragging rights if you could win the drag race at the stop light. Teenagers would only look at each other, and the challenge was on.

The Plymouth Barracuda, the Shelby Mustang Cobra, the Dodge Charger, the Chevy Camaro SS, the Pontiac GTO, the Chevelle SS 396, and the Oldsmobile Cutlass 442 were cars to watch. They were equipped with engines with as much as 450 horsepower, a stick shift, and a beautiful voluptuous vixen wearing a tight sweater in the passenger bucket seat, if you had any game. Having fun was having the right car and parking with the right girl, on the right night, at the right place, and the right song playing on the radio.

27. Which president of the United States began the construction of the Interstate Highway System?
    A) Dwight Eisenhower
    B) John F. Kennedy
    C) Lyndon B. Johnson

A large part of teenage culture is owning a vehicle. Automobiles provided freedom and movement. You were cool if you had a "souped-up" car. A souped-up car was one that was modified for performance or looks. Not me, I just wanted mine to run.

My vehicles were muscle cars in a way because they were always breaking down and required my muscles to move them. I will describe them in verse though I once described them in curse.

1953 Plymouth Cambridge, light green body, dark green roof, and a rusty hood.
Crusin' to school in my '53
Taking the back roads so no one could see
Is that him? They would ask
I parked my Plymouth and took off my mask

1955 Mercury Monterey, light green with a flat-head V-8 engine
My muscle car was a little slow
Without my muscles it wouldn't go
I pushed and cursed along the way
If I didn't, my car would stay

1955 Chevy Bel-Air, blue and white
My '55 Chevy was very cool
I parked it on the front row at school
The 3 o'clock bell, time to depart
My '55 Chevy wouldn't start
Johnny-Giovanni

1960's automobiles were so popular, they were immortalized in songs. Ronnie and the Daytonas sang about their *Little GTO,* the Beatles exclaimed, *Baby, You Can Drive My Car,* and John Kay of Steppenwolf sang about driving on the highway. He was *Born to be Wild.* The great Chuck Berry drove around with, *No Particular Place to Go* and Commander Cody described in detail his *Hot Rod Lincoln.* Not so happy songs of automobiles were Jan and Dean cautioning us about *Dead Man's Curve,* and J. Frank Wilson agonizing over his lost love in an automobile accident in *Last Kiss.*

With fast cars came fatal crashes. My good friend Don was killed in a single car crash when he was 23 years-old. Cultural icon James Dean was killed in a car crash September 30, 1955. He had only made three films in his short movie career when he died at the age of twenty-four. In 1976, Kiss wrote *Detroit Rock City* as a tribute to a fan killed on his way to a Kiss concert.

Chapter 16

Women's Rights, Women's Wrongs and Barbie

I might get some hate from both genders on this next topic, but I mean no harm. In the early Sixties, scores of women became dissatisfied with their unequal status. They received lower pay and fewer opportunities than men and believed they should be equal politically, economically, and socially. Right on! With the Industrial Revolution in the early 1800s, men went to work while women tended to the house and children. Most people believed that the home was the proper place for women. Women were viewed as more moral and charitable than men, therefore, better served to raise children. This is voiced in many courtrooms around the nation in divorce and child custody cases every day.

Personally, I have found most women are pleasant to be around, work with, and socialize with. Most are extremely caring towards their families. In 1963, a young singer named Lesley Gore recorded the song, *You Don't Own Me*, and it changed my views a little. The song became very popular with the young girls and their view of how they were treated by their boyfriends. Even if they were being treated well, they jumped on the bandwagon of this song. They wanted equal treatment and favorable treatment at the same time. That is also what I believe. Ladies are special and should be treated so.

Later, Helen Reddy contributed the song, *I Am Woman*. The song celebrated female empowerment. In my patriarchal Italian family, I saw the diminished status of women. Many times it crossed the line, and I felt anger and sorrow for the Italian ladies and children who were victims of behavioral abuse by their Italian husbands and fathers. I assured myself that I would never be that way.

I recall three women who tested my beliefs about women. Beth was a beautiful young girl that I had unsuccessfully pursued. She had a reputation of using unsuspecting victims, but in my case, I was a willing victim. Her friend warned me to beware. She often went on dinner dates and ordered large portions so she could have a quality leftover meal the next day. Men wanted to lavish her with gifts in hopes that they might be "the one" to win her charms. I knew all of those things, but I was still in pursuit. My infatuation had not been sufficiently diminished, but it was inevitable that the time would come.

She hinted once that she had no plans for Friday night. I swallowed the bait when she added, "I guess I'll just stay home and watch television." Undoubtedly, a television set that was given to her as a gift in the apartment that someone else was paying for. Bursting with anticipation, I eagerly, but casually, mentioned, "If you don't have any special plans, would you like to go out to dinner?" Her answer "yes" resonated in my ears like Beethoven's Fifth Symphony. "Da Da Da Dumm." I was going to defy the odds.

We went to a very nice restaurant, and as I had been forewarned, she ordered a sizeable meal certain to have leftovers. If I had had any amorous competence, I could be sharing those leftovers with her after my overnight stay. After dinner, I took her to a luxury lounge for music, dancing, and drinks. On the drive home, she saw a car she recognized at a beer joint and asked if we could go in. Of course, I said, "Yes." The surprise ending was about to take place.

She began talking to a person that I recognized. She walked over to me and asked, "Would you mind if Erik takes me home?" Let's recap, expensive dinner, leftovers, drinks, dancing and an empty wallet. Pretending to be unfazed, I said, "No problem." As I walked away, she acknowledged, "I really did have a nice time." All was not lost, because I knew Erik, and he was Italian. I hope their daughter has a Roman nose and unmanageable curly hair. I also enjoyed the leftovers she had forgotten in my car.

My second encounter with a boastful woman happened early in my teaching and coaching career. A teacher named Lou also worked at the school where I was employed. She liked to verbally show off and belittle men in a clever way, especially when other women were around. I was coaching the freshmen football team, and some of my players were in Lou's English class. Whenever she had a behavior problem with one of my players, she would always tell me, insinuating that my players lacked discipline in the classroom because of me. That was a sly way of accusing me of caring only about football and nothing else. Coaches hear that complaint all the time. One afternoon, Lou was in the library talking to the librarians, who were also her friends. I walked in to return some items that I had borrowed. Immediately, she brashly said, "Hey, Coach, I need to see you about a kid." The tone of her voice and abruptness pissed me off. I knew what she meant, but my wisecrack reply was, "No, thank you, I don't want to have a kid with you." She stood in embarrassing silence while the librarians tried unsuccessfully to muffle their laughter. Later, I regretted making that remark. Lou was just an insecure woman attempting to hide it through a boisterous, bogus personality.

My final confrontation with an annoying feminist woman was a young lady named Linda. Linda had the good looks and liked very much the adulation that came with them. It was difficult to get a date with Linda. Once I called her, and she asked me to come over to her house. When I arrived, no one was home. She probably had gotten a better offer after our conversation. Maybe she was feeling some sympathy for me after that put down, so on another occasion she gave me a call and said we could go out if I still wanted to. That wasn't too firm of an assurance, but again I fell to the temptation of being alone with Linda.

When I arrived to pick her up for the date, she proceeded to tell me she had gone shopping and bought the special outfit she was wearing just for me--tight fitting designer jeans, an almost transparent red blouse with red sequins, leather boots, and an intoxicating fragrance. Let the games begin.

We first went out to dinner, and she was basking in the glory of the attention she was getting from others. Again, I questioned myself for accepting this humbling display of flirtations with the public. At the restaurant, I had asked Linda in advance what she wanted to order. I wanted to see if she was going to order a large meal with leftovers. She said she wanted a salad and of course had to compliment herself, saying she wanted to keep her weight down and her body looking good. She excused herself to go to the restroom. I was getting the feeling she really didn't want to be with me. The waitress came to the table for our order and I said, "My date would like the house salad. She doesn't want to get fat." I continued looking at the menu, and the waitress helpfully asked, "Can I find something on the menu for you?" I said, "Yes, I'm looking for a better date than the one I've got." Playing along, the waitress said, "I can get off work early for you, but you will have to promise to take me home…in the morning." It did make me feel better, but Linda was about to make her return appearance to the table and to the patrons.

With no expectations on my part, the date actually improved. We finished dinner and went to listen to a local band. As we were driving home, Linda asked if we could go by my place and watch a movie. Was this girl falling to my charm or was this sympathy night?

Inside my house, I told her I was going to change into my movie-watching clothes: football-issued shorts and a coaching tee shirt. I did add that I had gone shopping that day also, but I didn't buy this outfit for her. I was trying to break the ice, but her ice was thicker than an Antarctic glacier. She asked if had a smaller size shorts and team tee shirt for her to wear. I went into the bedroom and found a size small shorts and a shimmel shirt. (A shimmel short is a half shirt that exposes the stomach area that players wear under their equipment.) In her typical self-absorbed way, she giggled, "These are too big." Sarcastically, I said, "Easier for them to fall off of you, my dear." She accepted that as a compliment. I said it out of desperation. I knew it was going to be my only date with her so there was no need for me to hold anything back.

With these pathetic remarks, I learned that if you lavished her with compliments, she was a lot more fun. We watched an old black-and-white suspense movie, *Double Indemnity*, with Fred Mac Murray and Barbara Stanwyck. We both were more interested in the movie than any romance, and I was glad. She was pretty and sexy, but her narcissistic nature was more than I wanted to accept. I personally prefer "fun dates" over "romantic dates" because those were the only ones I remember having. Then the fun began.

I put her new outfit that "she bought just for me "on a hanger and carried it to the car along with her boots. She was still wearing the football shorts and shimmel shirt. On the drive home we talked about the unforeseen captivating effect the old movie had on us. The end to a good date was just a few minutes away. What could disrupt this evening? I parked my car near the front door of her apartment. I picked up the hanger of her sexy clothes and boots to carry them to the door. I had no intention of going in. I didn't want to complicate or tarnish a joyful evening.

As she got out of the car, I saw a truck parked about four vehicles away with a man sitting in it. He opened the driver's side door. The dome light caught our attention and Linda looked at him and screamed, "RUN!" Linda ran first, trying to locate the keys to her apartment before she arrived at the door. Without a clue of what was happening, I jogged behind her, carrying her clothes and boots. I glanced back at the man following. He wore cowboy boots, tight jeans, a red plaid shirt with two pockets on the chest snapped closed with white pearl buttons, and a white cowboy hat. He was a cowboy, thankfully, without a horse or gun. He couldn't run very fast because of the tight jeans, and he was overweight. Linda found her keys, opened the door, and I followed in behind her. She closed the door quickly, and within a few seconds, the man was banging on the door.

I said, "I think that's for you."

He bellowed, "Open the damn door!"

I asked Linda, "Who is that?"

She confessed, "That's the man I'm engaged to." What was this poor cowboy thinking? Linda was wearing shorts and a shimel shirt, and I was carrying her clothes. He was crying at the door, "I love you, Linda." She answered through the door, "It's not what you think," while I sat on the couch thinking, "She's right, but he's not going to believe it."

They argued, he threatened me, she blamed me, and then they apologized to each other and spoke of marriage as I sat on the couch watching television. I was annoyed with the situation and with Linda. If not for her, this would not have happened. I was even more relieved because this was a harmless date, and I wasn't the one that had disrespected her boyfriend.

I asked her, "What is the cowboy's name?" She said, "Bubba." I hoped his posse of Tex, Slim, Roy, and Festus were not on the way. I told Linda, "Tell Bubba to go cool off in his truck because I want to go home. If not, I'm spending the night." Bubba looked harmless, but he did have a broken heart, the pieces of which could be used as a lethal weapon. I had watched enough true crime shows to be cautious.

After a while, she said Bubba had promised to sit in his truck until I left the complex. Good boy, Bubba. I was still not ready to forgive Linda. She opened the door and looked to confirm that Bubba was in his truck. I walked just outside the door turned to Linda and said, "Aren't you going to give me a good-night kiss?" Linda called me a string of unflattering profanities. I slowly walked to my car and yelled back, "You can keep the clothes!" Bubba's face was crimson, out shining his red truck. I decided Linda deserved one more insult since she blamed this on me so I taunted, "Hey, Linda, call me again sometime. I had fun." I made sure Bubba heard it. I waved as I drove off into the night, or in cowboy lore, "rode off into the sunset."

Do you think it was ironic that the Feminist Movement of the 1960s began around the same time as the debut of the most famous woman icon of all time, Barbie? I did some research about Barbie. Following is a brief history.

The Barbie Doll was the idea of Ruth Handler, whose husband was the co-founder of the Mattel Toy Company. Ruth and her husband, Elliot, had two children named, you guessed it, Barbara and Kenneth. Ruth thought it was important for the doll to have an adult body because no other doll on the market had one. Good idea, Ruth. Some parents were unhappy with the doll's distinct breasts. I think secretly the fathers thought the breasts were a good idea, but Barbie's were not big enough. As spoof, I mean proof, my research shows that if you place two Barbie dolls side by side, men pick up the one with the larger breasts first 100 percent of the time.

Barbie's Biography
Full Name: Barbara Millicent Roberts
Hometown: Willows, Wisconsin
Vital Statistics: 5'9," 110 lbs., 36-18-33
Status: Off and on relationship with Ken Carson
Pets: cats, dogs, horses, a panda, a lion cub, and a zebra

Vehicles: pink Corvette convertible, a Jeep, an airplane (she is a pilot and a flight attendant)

One of the most common criticisms of Barbie is that she portrays an unrealistic body image of a young woman. Critics say girls who tend to emulate her may become anorexic. In 1963, the outfit "Barbie Baby-Sits" came with a book entitled *How to Lose Weight,* which advised, "Don't Eat!" Another ensemble called "Slumber Party" in 1965, came with a bathroom scale permanently set at 110 lbs. In 1992, Mattel released "Teen Talk Barbie," who spoke the phrases "We will never have enough clothes, and I love shopping!" "Teen Talk Barbie" even said, "Math class is tough." With criticism from the American Association of University Women, in October of 1992, Mattel announced that "Teen Talk Barbie" would no longer say that phrase and offered a swap for anyone who owned a doll that did.

28. What Barbie became controversial to African-Americans?
   A) Oreo Fun Barbie
   B) McDonald's Barbie
   C) Antebellum Barbie

This research has led me to a possible new line of modern dolls, Garbie, Barbie's slutty sister. No harm intended, just fun. Presenting, the Garbie collection.

1) "You Don't Own Me Garbie"-- Just like the Lesley Gore song, this Garbie comes with an attitude. After playing with it once, you must pass it on to someone else, or Garbie will sing, *You Don't Own Me.*
2) "Ex-Wife Garbie"-- This doll comes with an attorney, the kids, the house, the car, alimony, a new wealthier husband, and anything else she wants.
3)" Implant Garbie"-- This version comes with two sets of boobs, a before and after set. This Garbie is popular among men.
4) "Female President Garbie"--Included are an array of pant suits and a shady past.

5) "Bill's Garbie—The set includes playmate dolls: Monica, Paula, Gennifer, and Dolly.
6) "Excuse Garbie--Ask her anything and she will answer one of the following: "I've got a headache," "I'm tired," "I don't have anything to wear," and finally, "No means no, you SOB!"
7) "Minority Garbie--This doll has a variety of ethnicities and colors, but all have the same Caucasian features of the original Barbie.
8) "Hefty Garbie"--This doll comes in a round box of candy.
9) "One Gender Garbie"--Two dolls. One looks like Garbie, the other looks like Ben. They're both Garbie!
10) "Senior Citizen Garbie--This age-defying Garbie looks just like Barbie did in 1959 but is really fifty-four years old.

And you thought Barbie was just cold, plastic, and had no heart!

Based on my findings, I have concluded that Barbie is the standard bearer for women. Not Susan B. Anthony (The "B" actually stands for Brownell. I was wrong all those years) not Elizabeth Cady Stanton, not Lucretia Mott, not Betty Friedan, not Gloria Steinem, and not Eleanor Roosevelt, or any other prominent females. These real-life women cannot match the influence on generations of young girls like Barbie has.

Let us not disrespect Ken, or is it let us disrespect Ben? Did you know Ken had a twin brother named Ben? Check out the Ben dolls.

1) "Child Support Ben"--This doll comes with an extra set of blue collar work clothes with real stains for Ben's second job so he can pay his outrageous child support.
2) "Laid-off Ben"--Ben hasn't had a job since in ten years and doesn't want one. Ben is well-dressed and happy, because he qualifies for unemployment, food stamps, worker's compensation, disability, tax relief, telephone assistance, Social Security, Medicaid, subsidized housing, home care assistance and government insurance. He also deals drugs on the side. This doll shouts "USA! USA!" His wardrobe includes the red, white and blue suit of Uncle Sam including the top hat. It represents the "new" American Dream.

3) “Transvestite Ben”--Ben has a large assortment of Garbie attire. You can only put these clothes on him from midnight until 6 A.M. or in the privacy of your room.
4) “Dead Beat Ben”--This Ben is adorned with dirty clothes, a four-day old beard, an ashtray filled with cigarette butts, and bad breath.
5) “I’m Not Italian Ben”-- He has two replaceable noses, one normal nose and one Roman nose. When he is with his Italian buddies, he wears his Roman nose, greases his hair back, speaks broken English and commits crimes. When he is with his WASP friends he wears the normal nose, a blonde wig, and speaks correctly.

Missing from this group is “Poor Bastard Ben.” It is no longer manufactured because of extremely low sales. Poor bastard.

29. What section of the Educational Amendments law prohibited federally-funded schools from discriminating against females in athletics?
A) Title VIII
B) Title IX
C) Title X

Chapter 17
The Abortion Dilemma

I am for equal rights for all Americans. I have worked for many women supervisors and never had a gender problem with any of them. I would be willing to help ANY person better himself or herself. Thus, my rant on Beth, Lou, Linda and Barbie was all in fun. I hope you understood and were not offended. If so, I sincerely apologize.

One of the most important goals for many women activists was the right to abortion. Until 1973, the right to regulate abortions was reserved for the states. "Jane Roe" had become pregnant by her boyfriend in 1969. She claimed to have been raped, thinking this would grant her a legal abortion. At the time, Texas law permitted abortions only to save the life of the mother.

Pro-abortion organizations used the case to challenge the Texas abortion law in court. The case reached the United States Supreme Court in 1973. The mother was referred to as "Jane Roe" to protect her privacy. Henry Wade was the Dallas County District Attorney who defended the Texas law. In its decision, the Supreme Court declared that all state laws restricting or limiting abortion were unconstitutional. After the *Roe v. Wade* ruling, pro-abortionists and pro-lifers still continue their disagreement today.

30. "Jane Roe" revealed herself to the press after the Supreme Court decision. Who is "Jane Roe?"
    A) Linda Coffee
    B) Sarah Weddington
    C) Norma McCorvey

I had one encounter with abortion. No, I wasn't the father, but I wanted to be. You say it best Maury, *"You are not the father!"* A young beautiful friend that I wanted to date became pregnant. Upon hearing the news, I called her, not knowing what kind of reaction she would have to my call about her condition. She confirmed the news. I asked her plans, and she didn't have any. She was considering all options. Wanting to be the option and wanting to be more than a friend, I made an offer. We could get married, and I would say the baby was mine. It was the Sixties, and anything was possible. Maybe my admiration for her and her friendship with me could develop into "living happily ever after." Even better, there was no chance the baby would look like me. I reassured her that we could make this happen. I talked, I pleaded, I counseled, and I prayed. I even offered to change my last name, but in the end, sadly, she chose abortion. She aborted me and kept her baby. Finally, an abortion story with a happy ending.

Abortion is a topic that confuses me. There are many ways to prevent pregnancies, but people allow it to happen anyway. It is a selfish act, when we don't consider the consequences of a possible pregnancy. If we know the facts in advance, abortion can be inconsequential. When it unexpectedly happens, we should show compassion to all involved, including the unborn. There is personal opinion, and there is public policy. Some people view abortion as a way of "dodging a bullet," while others view abortion as "firing a bullet." Whichever option you support, please be respectful and informed, set your differences aside, and pray for all involved. If interested, read *Diary of an Unborn Child*. The choice is yours.

Chapter 18
Trey

The Sixties carried forward with one life-changing episode after another. The Vietnam War had a hand in all of our lives. We all knew someone who served, and we all knew someone who had died while serving.

One who died from our school was a gifted athlete and quarterback on our football team. I first met Trey on a little league football team we played for when I was in the sixth grade. At that young age, it was easy to see he was going to be a great player. Trey played every sport in school. He was great on the hardwood floor of the gym in basketball, equally as good on the grassy diamond of the baseball field, and remarkable on the football gridiron. He was part of the folklore of WHS.

His family was more dedicated and supportive than any other. His father would often be at practice, and his family hosted many gatherings for the players at their home. They were friends to his teammates and treated us well. Trey was somewhat quiet and unamused by it all. Like the rest of us, he just wanted to have a good team and represent our school and classmates with his best effort. He was a classy teammate. How good was Trey? After his senior season, he received an athletic scholarship to LSU and went to Baton Rouge to be an LSU Tiger.

I don't know any details of his life at LSU other than he was on the football team and made some early appearances in some games. He left school and joined the Marine Corps and was deployed to Vietnam in October of 1967. He became a casualty of war on January 10, 1968. The name Henry Lee Prather III is engraved on Panel 34E, Line 24 of the Vietnam Memorial Wall. Thus, for all of his accolades on the hardwood, the diamond, and the gridiron, we can also add a hero on the battlefield. In a bizarre way, it was the only time that I envied Trey. What an honorable death.

To Trey and all of those that have sacrificed their lives for our country, I am eternally indebted.

Remembering Trey
Calling the play
Running the ball
Throwing the pass
Vietnam
The tragic newscast
Still today
Remembering Trey
Johnny-Giovanni

In addition to Trey, there were other members of our high school that were killed in the Vietnam War. Glenn Ogburn, Harold O'Neal, and Edward Cox. To commemorate them, there is a monument in the school square with their names inscribed. Each year on Veterans Day, they are deservedly honored with an assembly. I know those that attend now can't feel the emotion as we children of the Sixties. I wish we could do more for our deceased heroes than to pray and remember.

Chapter 19
Disgust and Hatred of the Vietnam War

The Vietnam War created bitter divisions in the United States. The government's intent was to prevent the spread of communism in Southeast Asia. That was the Cold War philosophy. Many young people protested America's involvement in the war and resisted the draft. They didn't accept that we were involved in a foreign war in a foreign land. Over 58,000 American soldiers died in Vietnam, and victory was never achieved. There is still resentment today by many Americans who lost family, friends, or loved ones in a war they deemed unnecessary.

Day after day, people saw images of wounded and dead American soldiers on the news. We checked the KIA (killed in action) section of the newspapers daily, hoping that we would not see a familiar name.

As the war escalated, government officials increased the draft. Many viewed the draft as unfair. College students were able to defer their military service until after graduation. Young men from low-income families were more likely to be sent to Vietnam because they were unable to afford college. American officials decided to increase the draft call, putting many college students at risk. An estimated 500,000 draftees refused to go. Some found ways to elude it. Others burned their draft cards, or fled the country. Some stayed and went to prison rather than fight in a war they opposed.

31. What famous athlete was convicted of draft evasion in June of 1967?
  A) Jim Brown
  B) Kareem Abdul Jabbar
  C) Muhammad Ali

Baby boomers had to decide how to fulfill their draft obligation in the 1960s. Their fathers, who had fought in World War II and the Korean War, were enthusiastic and willing to serve their country. Some even lied about their age so they could enlist early. They lived through the Great Depression and defended America in World War II. That is why they were called, “The Greatest Generation.” However, for Vietnam, many lied to resist the draft, and draft evasion was common. What title can we apply to them? Today, we have an all-volunteer military. What do you think the results of a draft law would be today?

32. How was the military draft changed to be more equitable during the Vietnam War?
    A) The names were chosen alphabetically.
    B) The names were chosen by a lottery.
    C) The legal draft age was changed to 21-31.

The 1960s became a season of violence in America. The division of the people and protests against the war had damaged the Democratic political party. President Lyndon Johnson stunned television viewers with his announcement, “I shall not seek, and I will not accept, the nomination of my party for another term as your President.” The man who replaced President John F. Kennedy, and had won the 1964 election of all things, was quitting.

In the spring of 1968, the media reported that an Army platoon under the command of Lieutenant William Calley had massacred twenty-two unarmed South Vietnamese civilians in My Lai. Most of the victims were old men, women, and children. Lieutenant Calley received a life prison sentence for the murders, but it was later reduced to twenty years.

In April of 1970, there was news that the United States had invaded Vietnam’s border country, Cambodia. This set off many protests of the United States widening the war. In May, at Kent State University in Ohio, National Guard troops fired on demonstrators, killing four and wounding nine others. Ten days later, police killed two students during a demonstration at Jackson State University in Mississippi. What was happening to our great nation? Societal divisions created issues neither our government nor our people could solve. Can it happen again?

In 1971, Daniel Ellsberg, a Defense Department worker, leaked the Pentagon Papers. The documents contained details of decisions that were made by the Presidents and their advisers without the consent of Congress. These papers also showed how the various administrations acted to deceive Congress, the press, and the public about the situation in Vietnam. The Pentagon Papers confirmed that our government had not been honest with the people. Is our government honest today?

On January 27, 1973, the warring sides signed an agreement ending the war.

33. Which United States President negotiated the end to the Vietnam War?
   A) Jimmy Carter
   B) Richard Nixon
   C) Gerald Ford

Chapter 20
Comprehending the Civil Rights Movement

The Civil Rights Movement of the 1960s had the biggest impact on America during the decade, and it still resonates today. Because of this movement, I think America is better off. This is not to say everything is good and the problems have been solved, because it is an ongoing process. I read and hear about discouraging events that have taken place and have even witnessed some during my lifetime. There have been positive and negative actions on both sides of this cause. These beliefs and feelings started long ago with the development of our nation. I'm not going to say I completely understand, though I try. Sometimes, I am probably wrong. Nevertheless, we all owe our existence to the same God, and I doubt that He would want us to be violent to each other.

34. What Supreme Court case legitimized segregation?
   A) *Plessy v. Ferguson 1896*
   B) *Schenck v. United States 1919*
   C) *Brown v. Board of Education 1954*

I did not comprehend segregation while growing up. I don't like writing in the terms of blacks and whites, because I don't think that way. My elementary school was all white but not my neighborhood, nor the parish Catholic Church where my family attended. African-Americans were attending our church in the 1960s. Our house was the second house on the left of my street. If I went outside and took a right past the first house and crossed the street, I would be in an African-American community. We waited at the same trolley stop, we went to the same neighborhood grocery, and we would wave to each other daily.

An elderly African-American woman came to our house about once a week. We called her Ms. Annie. She would knock on our door and ask my mother for some extra clothes, something to eat, or a couple of dollars. My mother always gave her something, and Ms. Annie would say over and over how much she appreciated it. That made me appreciate Ms. Annie. Then in her mismatched clothes and always a big hat, she would walk across the street to her house.

I often rode my bicycle to the neighborhood grocery and bought baseball cards or an RC Cola, or some giant Jack's cookies. If a neighbor of a different color was there, we would sit and talk. I would show him my baseball cards, or break off a piece of my cookie and give it to him, or share my bag of chips or drink. I never thought there was any difference. I did the same thing with my white friends. It was just being a boy.

It is refreshing for me today to pass an elementary school and see children of different races playing together on the playground or walking home side by side. They will assimilate into society with acceptance unless someone at home fills their minds with hate of the other.

Walking home from school, I would cut across the corner service station. An African-American man worked in the service bay changing oil in cars. I would shout a "Hey" to him, and he would smile, and return a "Hey." When we were at the same trolley stop going north to downtown, we would always strike up a conversation, mostly about sports. I was not aware of any discrimination going on. My parents never mentioned anything about racial differences. My father would buy barbeque in the heart of a minority neighborhood at a place called The Silver Moon because it was the best in town.

The nightly news broadcast showing police dogs, high pressured fire hoses, and police with riot sticks seemed like it was a movie. Movies are not real; the news was. I didn't have any animosity toward any race and didn't understand why some people did.

35. What action began the Civil Rights Movement?
   A) Nine African-American students attended Little Rock Central High School in 1957.
   B) Linda Brown sought admission to her neighborhood school in Topeka, Kansas, in 1950.
   C) Rosa Parks refused to give up her seat on a city bus in Montgomery, Alabama, in 1955.

At the time, our country resorted to violence in addressing civil rights issues. People were attacked, African-American churches were burned, protestors were removed with force from sit-ins, there was campus destruction, and hate filled the halls with the integration of Little Rock Central High School. Some people, both black and white, were murdered for the cause. In the Watts section of Los Angeles, thirty-four people were killed when a race riot broke out over police brutality. The level of hostility and rage entered our homes with the televised reports of Selma, Alabama

Dr. Martin Luther King, Jr., organized a demonstration for voting rights in Selma. As the protestors were marching out of Selma, the authorities ordered them to disperse. The marchers kneeled in prayer when state troopers and deputized citizens rushed the demonstrators with clubs and cattle prods. Demonstrators were beaten in full view of television cameras, stunning the nation with shocking film footage of the attack. Through this venue, many Americans were awakened to the plight of African-Americans.

While campaigning for the Presidency in 1960, John F. Kennedy promised to support the Civil Rights Movement actively. African-Americans responded by voting overwhelmingly for Kennedy. Their votes helped him narrowly win several key states. President Kennedy named several African-Americans to high-level positions in the federal government and appointed Thurgood Marshall to the Second Circuit Appeals Court in New York.

36. What position did Thurgood Marshall hold later in his life?
    A) Supreme Court Justice
    B) Vice-President
    C) Secretary of State

On August 28, 1963, more than 200,000 demonstrators of all races went to Washington, D.C. They gathered peacefully near the Lincoln Memorial, where Dr. King delivered a powerful speech about his dream of freedom and equality for all Americans.

The portion of Dr. King's "I Have a Dream" speech that is most often mentioned is the phrase, "not be judged by the color of their skin but by the content of their character."

I found out the truth of his statement one perfect April day. It was the ideal time to take my three "Star Wars" nerds from my spring driver's education class to the city streets to avoid some cars. I will call them George, Paco, and Murkel. Each weighed about one hundred pounds or less, and all three wore glasses. The four of us could easily fit in the front seat of the vehicle. That day, the driver's education car was to be a Naboo Royal Security Gain Speeder with one medium blaster cannon. I played along.

George, Paco, and Murkel felt at home. They put their light sabers in the trunk and off we drove into the Star Wars universe. I liked these students and was hoping for a successful day. Their driving was unexpectedly good, but the Star Wars references were dizzying to this humanoid. I decided to reward them with snow cones. We drove up to the small snow cone stand which had parking for only about three cars. We occupied the last space on the left. I bought our snow cones, and we sat at a picnic table under a tree. We talked and laughed. It may have been the latest and farthest these guys had ever been away from home after school.

It was Murkel's time to drive, and we got back in the car. Murkel was at the controls, with George and Paco in the back seat. I heard some loud music and turned to my left to see a "pimped" car with mixed races of gang bangers moving as close as they could to the driver's side of our car. Their car was separated from our side door by a few inches. Murkel looked nervous, swallowed deeply and adjusted his glasses. There was no way to open the driver's side door. He looked at me with fright.

The gang bangers peered at us from their car. They saw three baby-faced, small, frightened boys and wanted to scare them. It worked. George and Paco exited through the passenger side back door and ran to the Circle K convenience store on the corner. I remained in the car with Murkel in the driver's seat. The gang bangers got out of the car and walked up to the snow cone stand.

I told Murkel to sit tight and I would ask them to move their car. I was going to try and befriend them. I approached them and said, "Good job guys. You just scared two of my drivers' right out of the car. Can you please move your car so my other student can back out?" No response. I didn't want to escalate the issue, so I walked away. Would we need our light sabers?

We could wait for them to move, but that was not going to happen. I went back to the car, and Murkel had the doors locked. I tapped on the window for him to let me in. I opened the door and told Murkel to go to the Circle K with George and Paco, and I would pick them up there. Out of left field Murkel said, "I'm not going to leave you Coach, I got your back." ("Not judged by the color of their skin but by the content of their character.") This frail wisp of a teen had the gonads to stay and face the uneven odds. Did he realize the possible danger?

I told him to get out of the car. He slid across the seat and moved outside. I angled back into the car behind the wheel, and Murkel followed into the front passenger seat beside me. I began to maneuver the car slowly back and forth to create enough space to back all the way out. Trying hard not waiver Murkel said, "I'll keep my eyes on them, Coach." I freed the car from the narrow space and drove to the Circle K to retrieve George and Paco.

As I drove away from the store, the pimped car of gang bangers began to follow behind us. I told George and Paco not look back because the gang bangers were still playing their game of fear. No problem there because their eyes were closed and they were slumped down in the seat. I also ordered them to stay in the car if we had to stop. I drove toward the school because there was always activity going on there. I glanced in the rearview mirror to see how long our " new friends" would follow us. Each time I made a turn, they remained behind us, and Murkel would say, "Enemy still at six o'clock Coach." I was hoping he wouldn't use our medium blaster cannon on these thugs. We only had one.

Murkel voiced he had a plan. George and Paco were frozen in the back seat. I told him I was in charge, and the plan was to get them back safely to planet Mommy. We arrived at school, and I parked next to the SRO officer's patrol car. As we stopped, I asked if anyone needed a chill pill. They all laughed, "Aw, Coach, we had those hoodlums in our laser sight the whole time." That made me feel at ease. Murkel confessed that he had never been in a fight before. That revelation was no surprise. What do you think their version of the story is today, decades after the fact? Even I would like to know how they saved their driver's education instructor from the clutches of evil.

As a football coach, content of character plays a large role in the success of a player on your team. The biggest, fastest, strongest, and most talented are not always the best players. Character not only applies to sports but to all arenas of life. The best students are not always the smartest, the prettiest girl is not always the best date, the most educated teacher doesn't always do the best job of teaching, and the most expensive house will not ensure happiness, and you can continue on and on.

We all have dreams for our country and our families. These dreams will be difficult to achieve unless all races, religions, genders, and factions unite against injustice and unlawfulness and do their part to raise our personal standards and to improve all of humanity. I'm not spinning cotton candy here, we can make it happen. We spend too much effort on trying to win the argument rather than acknowledging the problem and trying to correct it.

By the late 1960s, the Civil Rights Movement had separated into dissenting groups. To many young African-Americans, progress was too slow. There was a call for black power and more violent action in contrast to Dr. King's non-violent approach. The idea of black power was popular in poor urban neighborhoods where many African-Americans resided. Black power emphasized racial distinctiveness, and many African-Americans showed their pride by adopting Afro hairstyles, African-style clothing, and taking African names. The Black Panther Party began in the bay area of Oakland and San Francisco.

37. Whose non-violent philosophy influenced Dr. Martin Luther King, Jr.?
    A) Buddha
    B) Abraham Lincoln
    C) Mahatma Gandhi

Dr. King went to Memphis, Tennessee, to support a strike by African-American sanitation workers. On the evening of April 4, 1968, Dr. King was assassinated as he stood on the balcony of the Lorraine Motel. National mourning came to the nation and riots broke out. The Civil Rights Movement continued, but it lacked the unity and vision that Dr. King had provided. An era had come to an end.

38. Who confessed to killing Dr. Martin Luther King Jr.?
   A) James Earl Ray
   B) David Duke
   C) Jim Jones

39. Other than John F. Kennedy, Robert Kennedy, and Dr. Martin Luther King Jr., what other assassination occurred in the turbulent 1960s in the United States?
   A) Governor George Wallace of Alabama
   B) Black Muslim Malcolm X
   C) Justice Thurgood Marshall

During my first teaching job, I thought everyone had the same goal as I did. Even better, I should say I thought I had the same outlook as others. Teach the students, be a good faculty member, support your school, and share with your co-workers. When I received my first teaching assignment, it was American History and Civics.

At the new teacher orientation, I sat with an African-American teacher, Mr. Brown. As we talked, I learned he had been transferred to the school because of the new integration law. He also told me he taught American History for seven years, and he had a master's degree. We compared teaching schedules, and I learned he was assigned to teach World Geography. Not knowing the consequences of my offer, I said, "Mr. Brown, since you are experienced in teaching American History and this is my first job, I don't mind changing schedules with you."

Thinking I was doing a good deed, I went to see the principal about changing teaching assignments with Mr. Brown. I did not know the principal didn't want Mr. Brown teaching American History. He had his reasons and that was not for me to question. He was the principal, and yet I thought I would be complimented for being a team player, allowing a teacher with more experience and a higher degree to have a choice in what he wanted to teach.

From that moment on, I was perceived as being on the wrong side of the issue. I did my best to show all teachers and students that I had no problem with the new integration law. I ate lunch with my new faculty friends and sat with them at faculty meetings, not realizing that it mattered to some. I was a new teacher to the school just as my new African-American co-workers were. I had no preconceived plan or agenda. I was just trying to be a friend.

Someone drew the conclusion that I was trying to be black. The next year I was transferred to an African-American junior-senior high school. One of my friends told me the word on campus by a supervisor was, "If he wants to be with the n______ he can be with all of them."

I reported to my new job with the same philosophy I had at my first job. I talked with the principal, a thirty-year veteran educator. The school was formerly under the "separate but equal" law (or Jim Crow laws), and he had been the principal during segregation. We talked for a short time. I assume he was trying to ascertain if I really wanted to be there. Later we talked formally about education and the changes the nation was experiencing. He presented me with my teaching schedule--American History! He had no qualms about a white man teaching a class of African-Americans about American history. I appreciated his trust, and his kindness invigorated me to do the very best at my new school.

Why did an African-American principal at an African-American school approved of a young white man to teach what was taking place in America about his race? Did he really believe that I could succeed, or was he setting me up for failure? Did he want to show me a view of history that I couldn't learn in any college classroom? Was I a pawn in a cruel game of "Gotcha?"

Most of the students were respectful and accepting. The early questions I was asked had nothing to do with race relations or the status of America. Instead, the students asked, "Can I touch your hair?" "Do you think I'm pretty?" "Can I sit with you at lunch?" And the standard classroom question, "Do we have to do this?" It was obvious that some of these students had never been around a white person. Thus, curiosity far exceeded animosity. Some would come to class in the morning before the opening bell and ask, "What did you eat last night?" "What did you watch on television?" "Do you have a picture that I can have?" "How do I look today?" "Am I pretty?"

My department supervisor at the school was a lifetime educator who lived across the street from the school. I remember some early advice she gave me, "These children are not aliens. They have feelings of love, pain, and wanting to be accepted just like all children." So right she was.

There was a lot of potential sitting before me in class, but also a lot of issues: reading, writing, study habits, neglect, complacency, a lack of attentiveness, and no desire to learn. In most public schools across the nation, those problems still remain.

The supervisor, Mrs. Douglas, wanted to arrange an academic competition among American History classes. I was one of the American History teachers, and a very well-dressed disciplinarian, Mr. Stall, was the other. Mr. Stall taught the enriched class, and I taught the regular education students. The main difference in enriched and regular education was the commitment of the students. Our competition was based on a television show called the College Quiz Bowl.

Teams of students from two colleges would face off in an academic competition by answering questions from a moderator. Mrs. Douglas informed me to get a team of four of my best students ready. Our opponents were the best students from Mr. Stall's classes. The competition was to be held in the auditorium as part of an assembly to promote academics.

I selected my best four, and two were very good. The only reason they were not in the enriched class was because of their discipline record. The enriched classes did not accept students that were disruptive. We prepared thirty minutes before school every day, and Mr. Stall had his team practice after school without time restrictions. I tried the after-school approach once, but my team didn't show up. I guess they had other things to do.

Fortunately, my team was not deterred by going against those thought of as the best students in the school. We changed our team name from 'Habitual Underachievers" to "Born Again Academicians." Our epiphany came one session when I was teaching about popular presidential elections. In the 1948 election, the *Chicago Tribune* printed the headline, "Dewey Defeats Truman." The polls had projected that Thomas Dewey would defeat Harry Truman. When the votes were counted, however, Truman had won the election. We looked at a picture of the headline, and I told my team, "Everyone in school expects Mr. Stall's team to win the competition. They are Dewey but we are Truman. We will win." My team erupted with confidence and the will to learn.

On assembly day, the students filled the auditorium in anticipation of our defeat. My team had become so confident that they were trash talking everyone. I didn't advise them against it because I didn't want to lessen their enthusiasm about the competition or their belief that they could win. The "Born Again Academicians" were saying things like, "What competition? No competition!" "Are you sure they are going to show up?" "Call the police; there's going to be a beat down," and "Can we celebrate on stage after we win?" It reminded me of my football arrogance in school. I loved my team.

The curtain opened, and Mrs. Douglas introduced herself as the moderator, and she introduced Mr. Stall and me. I heard one member from my team say, "Mr. Stall*?* I call him Ms. Stall." From that comment, I knew we were ready to rumble. Then, Mrs. Douglas introduced the teams. Of course, Mr. Stall's team was the crowd favorite and received the loudest ovation. My team even had a smattering of boos, but I knew all of those students who were suspended wanted us to win. They just couldn't be in attendance.

My team got off to a slow start, and we were behind early. I am going to use the excuse we were too hyped up. We answered some questions and closed the gap in the score just before intermission. I told my team one thing: "Truman is going to defeat Dewey."

As the contest resumed, my team was ready. We were the first to answer on five straight questions. The auditorium joined in the momentum shift and began cheering for the underdog. Mr. Stall's team became introverted (like the personality of many good students). They rang in to answer a question, but they were incorrect. Our team rushed to the opportunity to answer the same question with the correct response. We were going in for the kill. From that point on, Mr. Stall's team did not attempt to answer another question. Their more fragile personalities had taken over. The "Born Again Academicians" had triumphed on the big stage.

My team members received their trophy and with a nod of my head, well, many nods of my head, they went to show proper respect to their opponents. Would success spoil us? After the victory, we returned to class. George asked if he could smoke a victory cigar. He wasn't kidding, therefore, I had to say no. Mr. Stall still had the better students in the enriched classes, and my team reverted back to their previous name "Habitual Underachievers." Most students can achieve when the right reward is dangled in front of their face. But for one moment in time, we achieved our potential.

The following school year, my third as an educator, Mrs. Douglas asked me if I would teach a group of enriched seventh graders. The plan was to take the thirty best students coming into the school and provide them with an enrichment program guided by a team of select teachers. I worked with the math teacher, the science teacher, and an English teacher, and we coordinated our lessons as closely as possible. We went on field trips to different places of worship, we went to restaurants to sample different ethnic foods, we went to the courthouse to watch a trial, and toured different sections of the city, even the airport. We tried to expose this group to as many different places and experiences as we could in hopes that they would value education and America.

Two of that group became doctors; a young lady in the field of internal medicine and a young man that became a local pediatrician. Don't get the wrong impression. I'm not saying I know how to relate to African-Americans more so than others. I never looked at it as teaching African-Americans. They were students, and I taught all students the same, regardless of their differences or their effort. I taught them with respect.

Part Three

Answers 21-39

21. Who released the album *The Times, They are a-Changin'?*
   A) Bob Dylan
   They were many protest songs in the 1960s. As with Bob Dylan's *The Times, They are a-Changin',* the subjects were usually poverty, racism, the Vietnam War, and society. As a teacher, I once gave an assignment in my American History class to make a presentation of a 60s protest song and give an explanation of the lyrics. The assignment was a hit, just like Dylan's album.

22. Why were many people opposed to a Catholic president?
   C) If elected, his or her allegiance might be to the Pope.
   Our nation was founded on Protestantism. John F. Kennedy has been the only Catholic elected President of the United States.

23. One of the most popular hippie destinations of the Sixties was the Haight-Ashbury district. In what city is it located?
   C) San Francisco
   Haight-Ashbury was a popular hippie destination in San Francisco during "The Summer of Love" in 1967. Eventually the influx of people deteriorated the neighborhood into overcrowding, homelessness, hunger, drugs, and crime.

24. What was the defining feature of hippies?
   B) They had long hair.
   If your choice was to have longer hair, many thought you were a hippie. Most of America didn't approve of the hippie lifestyle. Schools and businesses developed hair-cut policies and dress codes for their students and employees. Even I was once forced to cut my hair at my first teaching job.

25. Which is a slang term for LSD?
A) Acid
Lysergic acid diethylamide is colloquially known as acid. It was a popular psychedelic drug in the 1960s. Users have described a "trip" as a dreamlike state where one sees fantastic shapes in kaleidoscopic colors. Dr. Timothy Leary of Harvard University was the most prominent LSD researcher in the United States and a hippie idol.

26. The original McDonald's mascot was a man with a chef's hat on top of a hamburger shaped head. Who was he?
C) Speedee
When the restaurant reorganized in 1948 and began selling hamburgers, it adopted production techniques which allowed for "speedy" service or "fast food." Speedee was replaced by Ronald McDonald in 1967.

27. Which president of the United States began the construction of the Interstate Highway System?
A) Dwight Eisenhower
The Federal Highway Act was passed in 1956 to construct forty thousand miles of interstate highway over the next ten years. It was in response to Cold War tensions to make the United States better prepared to move troops and equipment across the country in case of an attack.

28. What edition of Barbie became controversial to African-Americans?
A) Oreo Fun Barbie
Mattel had manufactured both a white version and a black version of the doll. Critics argued that "Oreo" is a derogatory term meaning "black on the outside but white on the inside. Mattel recalled the dolls, which have since become a collector's item. "Colored Francie" debuted in 1967 and "Christie" was released in 1968. The first Black Barbie was introduced in 1980. They can be found on eBay.

29. What section of the Educational Amendments law prohibited federally-funded schools from discriminating against girls and young women in athletics?
B) Title IX
The Educational Amendments were passed on June 23, 1972. Title IX states, "No person in United States shall, on the basis of sex, be excluded from participation in, be denied the benefit of, or be subjected to discrimination, under any education program or activity receiving federal financial assistance." Title IX has been a huge success for female athletes in high school, college, and the coaching profession. I don't see how anyone could be against this.

30. "Jane Roe" revealed herself to the press after the Supreme Court decision. Who is "Jane Roe?"
C) Norma McCorvey
Norma McCorvey gave birth to the baby in question, who was eventually adopted. The case took three years to reach the Supreme Court. In her 1994 autobiography, *I Am Roe,* McCorvey wrote of her lesbian sexual orientation and expressed remorse for her part in in the law suit. McCorvey then worked as part of the pro-life movement.

31. What famous athlete was convicted of draft evasion in June of 1967?
C) Muhammad Ali
Muhammad Ali was a gold medal recipient for the United States in boxing in the 1960 Olympics. The Supreme Court reversed his conviction in 1971 ruling his conscientious objection claim was religiously-based and sincere.

32. How was the military draft conducted during the Vietnam War?
B) The names were chosen by a lottery.
I will try to explain the lottery method. The days of the year, including February 29th, were assigned the numbers 1-366. The numbers were put in a plastic capsule and placed in a large glass container. The first number drawn was #258 representing

September 14th. All eligible men born on September 14th between the years 1944-1950 would be drafted first. The process continued for all 366 days if needed.

33. Which United States president negotiated the end to the Vietnam War?
    B) Richard Nixon
    Henry Kissinger was the chief U.S. negotiator in the peace talks. He emerged from the secret peace talks with North Vietnam to announce, "Peace is at hand," on October 26, 1972.

34. What Supreme Court case legitimized segregation?
    A) *Plessy v. Ferguson 1896*
    Homer Plessy was seven-eighths Caucasian and one-eighth African descent. A group of concerned citizens, trying to repeal the Louisiana Separate Car Act, persuaded Homer Plessy to participate in a test case. Plessy bought a first class ticket and boarded a "whites only" railroad car to participate in a test case. A private detective working with the Plessy group was hired to arrest Homer Plessy. Homer Plessy brought a law suit against the state of Louisiana, but Judge John Howard Ferguson ruled that the state had the right to regulate railroad companies as long as they operated within the state boundaries. The case went to the United States Supreme Court, which ruled 7-1 in favor of Louisiana. The ruling established the "separate but equal doctrine." Separate facilities for the two races were legal as long as they were equal. It was the beginning of two separate school systems, separate water fountains, separate bathrooms, separate movie theaters, separate hotels, etc.

35. Whose action began the Civil Rights Movement?
    C) Rosa Parks
    Rosa Parks refused to give up her seat on a city bus in Montgomery, Alabama, in 1955. After her arrest, African-Americans in Montgomery organized a boycott of the bus system. Mass protests

began, and many African-Americans decided the time had come to demand equal rights. This event opened the eyes of many people.

36. What position did Thurgood Marshall hold later in his life?
    A) Supreme Court Justice
    Marshall was chief counsel for the NAACP. His most famous accomplishment was representing the NAACP in the case *Brown v Board of Education.* Marshall became the first African-American to serve on the Supreme Court when appointed by President Lyndon Johnson in 1967.

37. Whose non-violent philosophy influenced Dr. Martin Luther King,Jr.?
    C) Mahatma Ghandi
    Nonviolent resistance was used by Ghandi to gain independence for India from the British. Gandhi acted against unjust British laws through protests. The protests brought attention and sympathy to the liberation of India.

38. Who confessed to killing Dr. Martin Luther King Jr.?
    A) James Earl Ray
    Dr. Martin Luther King Jr., was shot and killed in Memphis, Tennessee, on April 4, 1968. James Earl Ray was convicted on March 10, 1969, after pleading guilty. He later recanted his confession and tried unsuccessfully to gain a new trial. He died in prison on April 23,1998.

39. Other than John F. Kennedy, Robert Kennedy, and Dr. Martin Luther King, Jr., what other assassination occurred in the 1960s?
    B) Malcolm X
    Malcolm X became a symbol of the black power movement that swept the nation. Discouraged by the scandals of the Black Muslims, he broke from them in 1964. He criticized the organization and its leader, Elijah Muhammad. Three members shot and killed him in February, 1965, while he was giving a speech in New York.

Part Four

Football, Friends, and a Broken Heart

Chapter 21

Hail to the Game of Football

I have loved the game of football since the fourth grade. I played for the neighborhood little league team that had a weight limit of seventy-five pounds. I was a sixty-eight- pound wrecking ball willing to crash into any moving object. I loved the smell of the equipment, the feel of the grass, the sound of contact, and the cries of pain. What was wrong with me? When there was a skinned elbow or knee, our coach would say, “Rub some dirt on it. You’ll be alright.” His other standard line was, “Hit ‘em hard enough to leave a mark.” Our coach gained his football expertise while delivering mail.

He constantly smoked during practice but would always talk to us about conditioning at the end of practice between deep draws off his cigarette. We loved him because we were on a “real football team” with “real uniforms,” and we had a “real coach.” I would even call him a great coach because we were terrible, and he kept it from us the whole season. We lost every game except the last one, which was a 6-6 tie. What jubilation! I wish that I could see that after-game celebration again. We were screaming, hugging, and throwing our helmets as the referee indicated that the game was over. It was awesome not to lose. It was our first non-loss. That game was going to be my topic at show and tell on Tuesday at school.

My playing career progressed to the eighty-five pound team. We only lost one game. I came to understand the sports phrase “Act like you’ve been there before.” On the 105 pound team, I was on an average team, but we had great uniforms: blue pants with a gold stripe, matching blue shirts with gold numbers, and gold helmets. ZZ Top was right; every girl is crazy about a sharp dressed man. Once, my mother told me to put my best clothes out so she could iron them for church. I put out my blue and gold football uniform.

After that it was on to junior high school and my first jock strap. Our junior high school coach told us football regulations required that we must wear one. He never explained the purpose of it. He was the coach, and we didn't question him, just did as he instructed. Curiosity got the best of me so I had to ask, "Coach, how does a jock help you in football?" He said, "It keeps your family jewels safe in the vault." Another of our young players asked, "Coach, would someone really try to steal them in a game?"

Junior high school football was much different because there was no weight limit, and some of the players were up to two years older than I was. The best difference was other than parents at the games, there were cheerleaders and girls. Hearing those cheers and knowing people cared boosted me to do the best I could. If someone scored a touchdown, his name would be in the newspaper. This game was getting better and better.

We traveled by school bus to other junior high schools in the city. It was fun to drive up to a rival school and here the jeers and cutting remarks. It was more fun to check out the rival cheerleaders. My way of checking them out was during a play. I would stray right into their formation on the sideline. In one game, an opposing cheerleader took offense to my sideline caper. I saw the embroidered name on her sweater. Her name was Cindy. With disdain in her voice, she cried, "Who do you think you are?" I smiled and said, "The one who's going to score the next touchdown, and I am going to name it after you, Cindy Six." As I walked back toward the field, I felt her pom pom hit me in the back. She shouted, "Shame on you"! I countered, "Did you just say, 'fame on you'? You are soooo right!" Was it arrogance? Absolutely, just the way you draw it up.

My high school alma mater, WHS, had achieved extraordinary athletic success in the 1960s. The school opened in the fall of 1960 and concluded its first year in May of 1961. The football team did not win a single game in the inaugural season, but after that they were a powerhouse throughout the decade. The school won 111 games and seven district titles in the next thirteen years. Woodlawn was regularly in the playoffs, a state runner-up in 1965, and an undefeated state champion in 1968.

Our coaching staff was the reason for our success. They were a group of six men who instilled in us discipline, a work ethic, and self-confidence to compete against anyone, even the more talented.

The philosophy of practice was different at that time. There were no water breaks. The belief was players got in shape by depriving themselves of hydration. Hydration took place after practice. Preseason practice always began on August 15th and lasted for two weeks, the worst two weeks of the calendar year. They were called "two- a -days" because practice was from 8 A.M. to 10 P.M. in the morning and from 3 P.M until what seemed like the twelfth of never in the afternoon. This was in the humid Louisiana climate where the only place on earth that was hotter in the afternoon was the Sahara Desert.

Often, during the morning session, I would lick the dew from the grass for any source of water. The schedule never varied. Practice was always in full uniform and began with stretching, blocking drills, tackling drills, offensive drills, defensive drills, scrimmage, conditioning, and the sun going down.

On Thursdays we had the "Perfect Ten" drill. The perfect ten drill was neither perfect, nor ten. The team would start at the goal line for play one, then we would sprint ten yards to run the next play. The play only counted if all eleven players executed their assignment perfectly. If the team could run ten perfect plays that would cover the length of the 100 yard field, the drill would be over. At any time, if the play was not perfect, the team would start over again with play one at the goal line.

Usually, somewhere between plays four to eight, our offensive line coach would yell, "Not good enough. Start over." The perfect ten always ended up being the imperfect thirty plus. Sometimes gasping for air, I would say, "Hey, Coach, the only perfect ten is at her house waiting for me. Can we finish this up?" His standard reply was, "We need to get more serious about this." Then I would look toward Jack with a grin, and pretending to be serious, he would mouth the words, "I love you," trying to make me laugh. "Is that serious enough, Coach?" We were getting really serious or really delirious.

Our head coach was the perfect man, soft spoken, intelligent, and not an asshole like some of the others. He was too much of a gentleman to berate a player, unlike two of the other coaches who performed that task with exceptional cruelty and glee. He taught math and had played for LSU. He could analyze and find the weaknesses of our opponents and prepare an excellent game plan each week. He was well-respected by the entire team and staff, and today, is in the Louisiana Sports Hall of Fame. All I wanted from him was an "Atta boy."

One of the assistant coaches served with the United States Marines in the Korean Conflict. He was tall and slim, and as he walked to the practice field, he would flip his cigarette to the side as the smoke escaped on its own from the corners of his mouth. He was a tough guy times ten. One practice, I was not having a good day, and I was making a lot of mistakes. He walked by me and said, "The only place you should start is in the concession stand selling popcorn." The only time he would smile was if someone was in pain. His pet phrase was "All right, girls." We all knew it was just an act for our behalf. We loved him as much as we did the other coaches.

One night Jack, Don, and I were looking for something to do. Don suggested we go to a bar near his house because they gave free popcorn and peanuts when you ordered a beer. We knew the free popcorn and peanuts was an excuse, but we all went to the 171 Club. Boys will be boys. We entered the darkened establishment and took a table near the door a few feet from the bar. We wanted to be near the exit if things went wrong.

We ordered three beers and served with them were the popcorn and peanuts. Don, being Don, asked the waitress if she was old enough to work there. She gave us a disgusted look, knowing we were high school guys trying to be cool. I asked her how much for the beers and she said, "Nothing. They were paid for by the tall slim man at the bar." We looked over, and Coach smiled and said, "Hello, girls." We had been caught. Don suggested that we let him take the blame, and Jack and I wholeheartedly agreed. We chugged down the beers quickly and left the popcorn and peanuts. As we were leaving, Don said, "Hey, Coach, we won't tell anybody we saw you here." Coach never mentioned it at school. Love is a kindhearted coach, a few beers, and the man code of silence.

We had some great football players. The 1965 state runner-up team was led by quarterback, Terry Bradshaw. Terry went to college at Louisiana Tech and played in the NFL for the Pittsburgh Steelers, winning four Super Bowls. He was inducted into the NFL Hall of Fame. The undefeated 1968 state championship team was directed by quarterback Joe Ferguson. Joe played his college football at the University of Arkansas and played fourteen years in the NFL. He was the starting quarterback for the Buffalo Bills for ten years. Another WHS quarterback, Billy Laird, class of 1962 and Louisiana Tech class of 1966, was drafted by the then Boston Patriots (today's New England Patriots). Put the great Trey Prather in that group of quarterbacks and that would be four outstanding quarterbacks in the 1960s at WHS. There were many other prominent WHS players of the 1960s who went on to play college football.

Friday night the lights were bright
People would cheer the band would play
Our red and blue
Was on display
Johnny-Giovanni

Playing football on Friday nights for Woodlawn High School was one of the great experiences of my life. My most glaring personal problem (that only I knew) was I hated to lose. Losing was not being good enough all over again. It has consumed me since those sandlot days when my brother and cousin would hold me down after a loss until everyone went home. After one of our few losses in high school, we were displaying the sportsmanship that our coaches and administrators felt was an obligation. To them, sportsmanship was the most important thing. Maybe it was to them, but not to me. I would fake it most of the time.

After one game, one of the adversaries from the other team reached his hand out to me for a post-game handshake. Overcome by the loss, I told him, "You can put that hand in your pants and spend some quality time with your chubby." Disastrously, one of our coaches overheard my remark. He rightly reprimanded me on the spot and said to report to him the next morning at school.

We always had some light running and a film session on Saturday morning after a Friday night game. After the running session, the coach told me I had some additional running for my unsportsmanlike display after the game. It was called the whistle drill. He would blow the whistle, and I would run. On the next whistle, I would walk; then another quick whistle, and I would run again. This continued for about thirty minutes. Every time I would pass him, he would say, "Think about what you did." I did not feel any regret in what I said. The more I ran, the more I was convinced that I was defending the honor of our school, our team, our colors, and our classmates. We had let them down by losing. I would have fought their entire team if necessary.

Losing embarrassed me. It was just another reminder that I was a failure. I still have animosity today for some schools, and I always will. Coach Red Sanders of UCLA and Coach Vince Lombardi of the Green Bay Packers both said, "Winning isn't everything. It's the only thing." Coach Sanders, when asked by a reporter of the rivalry with the University of Southern California, said, "It's not a matter of life and death. It's more important than that." I believed what they said. Don't misunderstand. I'll take responsibility for myself and say that is how I felt during practice, a game, whether it be playing or coaching, right or wrong. I could never completely rid myself of that feeling. I could

world would be a better place.

He was a military officer, he made Khrushchev blink first during the Cuban Missile Crisis, he said we would land a man on the moon and we did, he assured the people of West Germany in his speech *Ich bin ein Berliner* (I am a Berliner) that the United States would support them after the construction of the Berlin Wall, and he liked to play touch football and have large family gatherings. John F. Kennedy served the United States as President for a little more than 1,000 days. His approach to governing and his captivating personality persuaded many people all over the world to believe in him.

Disclosures about Kennedy's philandering and his reliance on pain killers to hide his health problems emerged years after his death. Those disclosures tarnished his image. Nevertheless, he is frozen in my mind at age forty-six as a handsome, personable, intelligent, witty president fit for the 1960s.

Accused presidential assassin Lee Harvey Oswald was shot dead in the Dallas Police Station two days after the assassination of President Kennedy.

40. Who was the gunman that shot and killed Lee Harvey Oswald?
   A) Bar owner Jack Ruby.
   B) Dallas Police Officer J.D. Tippet.
   C) Agent Gerald Behn, chief of JFK security.

41. How many United States presidents have been assassinated while in office?
   A) Two
   B) Three
   C) Four

There was indecision if our game should be played that night. With all the preparation and travel teams had done, the officials decided that we would play. Game time was 7 P.M. Already playing with the grief of a dead President, our team saw the New Orleans skies open up with torrential rain. Once the game started, the day's events were lost in the struggle for playoff survival. Our opponents that night had an All-State offensive tackle named Paul Albato. Paul was 6'6" and weighed 280 pounds, according to the scouting report. In the game program, he was just listed as a #78 a big, mean SOB.

Our defensive scheme was called a 5-4, meaning we had five defensive linemen, two inside linebackers, two safeties, and two cornerbacks. I was an inside linebacker, usually lined up across from the opposition's offensive guard. Our defensive coordinator called a 5-4 Eagle, meaning the inside linebackers would widen out over the offensive tackle. What was he thinking? That was where I met Paul Albato aka Bigfoot.

I was 5'10"; and when I squatted down in a linebacker's stance, I was about 4'10." Paul was 6' 6"; and when he got into his three point stance, he looked as if he was still 6 '6." I lined up in front of him and looked up at his face, not a friendly sight. I tried to stand up taller in my stance so we could be nearer in height. At the snap of the ball, Paul hit me so hard, I thought my water broke. He drove me back into the secondary a few miles from home, and I lay on the ground, my body vibrating like a tuning fork. As I picked myself up off the ground, our coach had already sent in a replacement for me.

I jogged to what I hoped was the sideline and my body was still convulsing. My coach said, "You're standing up too much in your stance." I said, "How could you even see me in front of that sonofabeast?" He sent me back into the game, but now I had a plan. I thought if his name was Albato, he must be Italian, and I could get on friendly terms with him. As he came out of the huddle and jogged up to the line of scrimmage, I greeted him with, "Hey Paul, I'm Italian, too." Paul answered, "How should I know that?" I said, "Look at my Roman nose." Paul said, "I thought you said you were Italian, you little Roman bastard. Shut up and play football or you'll be picking your Roman nose up off the ground." Suffice to say, Paul was no student of foreign countries, but he was a great offensive tackle who could cause an unexpected bowel movement anytime he hit you. The game program was accurate. Number 78 was a big, mean SOB.

The game ended in a 7-7 tie. The tiebreaker was the team with the most first downs would be declared the winner. They had 6, and we had 5. Under better conditions, I think we would have won, but I always think like that. We never lose. Occasionally, time runs out when we are behind, but I know if we had kept playing, we would have won eventually. I learned that from Vince Lombardi when I was growing up. It was the greatest excuse of all time.

Saturday following the Friday night tie, which went into the record book as a loss, we packed our gear for the last time that season. On the way home, we stopped in Baton Rouge and watched the LSU-Tulane football game. It was therapeutic to sit in Tiger Stadium with Jack, Mitch, Don, and Thomas, watch the game, and console each other before the melancholic journey home.

Once back home, I was invited for a weekend visit to Northeast Louisiana University. When I arrived in Monroe for my visit, my teammate and I were provided a room in a nearby motel. One of their current players served as our host to show us around campus, and of course, the night life of the city.

I was more dazzled by the coed show on campus. The Northeast girls were foxy, good-looking, and enthralling. After seeing them, I was ready to sign on the dotted line. I followed one very cute, very small, Chinese girl wearing a tight, wicked, black leather mini-skirt and a tight, yellow sweater. Her dark red lipstick outlined perfect lips, and the make-up that accented her Asian eyes and high cheek bones had me mesmerized. Her lustrous, black, Asian hair framed an exceptionally beautiful face. I was hungry for Chinese. I decided on my major right then, foreign relations. I was about to lose my equilibrium when Scottie beamed me back to reality. She met up with a guy who put his arm around her, and they strolled to class. I was thinking, "Lucky American bastard." Then I remembered, I was just a visiting, dumb high school jock.

The following weekend, Mitch and I received an invitation to Northwestern State University. I couldn't get Northeast or the vision of the Chinese beauty out of my mind. We met the coaches and some of the players from our hometown. They put us up in the dorm, and we visited the campus Saturday morning. It was an old campus but very scenic.

Northwestern was located in a small town and had an honored reputation as a teachers preparatory college. It would have been a good place to go to school, but NLU had won me over.

I canceled a visit to Southern Arkansas University because my mind was made up. I wanted to be an NLU Indian. Through my commitment and NLU's guidance, I became a college graduate. I still visit NLU intermittently. I recount from the NLU experience, that education is an ongoing process throughout life. It must be advanced continuously.

Chapter 22
Hope, a Dream, and a Kick in the Groin

Sitting with the one I love
Beneath the night sky above
Thinking the unthinkable
Johnny-Giovanni

The Christmas holidays were approaching, and there would be a lot of time away from school to share with that special girl for the occasion, but I was companionless. Every Jack needs a Jill during Christmas. Even a Guido needs a Guidette. I was a lonely boy, all alone with nothing to do.

I was recovering emotionally and physically from a long football campaign. My friend and teammate, Warren, called me to see if I was interested in a double date to a nearby city for the Christmas Festival. It became a life changing event. I can remember looking at the calendar and seeing the date, Saturday, December 7. For me, dating history was made. Warren was dating a very pretty cheerleader. I told him I'd like to go, but I didn't have anyone to take. He suggested a very pretty classmate named Jan. Not the previous Jan, the enchanting Aphrodite, the masterpiece of perfection Jan, but another Jan that would silently gain possession of every emotion that I possessed and those that I didn't know I had. All I was expecting was a night out with my teammate, his girlfriend, and a beautiful girl that I didn't know.

The date began like all other dates. We picked up the beauties and made the one-hour drive to Natchitoches. We strolled along the river bank, ate some festival treats, watched the fireworks display, held hands, and talked. I didn't anticipate any connection from someone I had known for only three hours. On the drive home, Warren's girlfriend wanted to stop and see the old private school she had previously attended in Natchitoches. Warren located the school and off they went sightseeing. I sat in the car talking to Jan; then, she got a little closer. Startlingly, she kissed me. The Christmas Festival fireworks were colorless and silent compared to Jan's kiss. That kiss awed me with an endless array of colorful confusion in my mind. My temperature went up to 110 degrees and my hormones raged out of my body. *Yes, Virginia, there is a Santa Claus!*

42. Where did the phrase *Yes, Virginia, there is a Santa Claus* come from?
    A) A speech by the 26th President Theodore Roosevelt in 1902.
    B) An editorial by reporter Francis Church in the *New York Sun* newspaper in 1897.
    C) The last words of comedian W.C. Fields, who died on Christmas Day, 1946.

The first date with Jan was awesome, the second date amazing, the third date incredible. On some weekends, we didn't go out because Jan had to stay with her two younger sisters. Those were the best weekends of my life. Her mother was a single mom, a professional business woman and sometimes away from home. I admired her for the way she administered her life running a business school and raising three beautiful young daughters. I would visit with Jan and her sisters, and they became trustworthy friends. I had hoped to belong to the family of these three wonderful young ladies one day.

That winter, Christmas in our area received one of its largest snowfalls ever, as if it was a special Christmas gift from nature for Jan. I presented my gifts to Jan one cold Christmas vacation night. We sat in the car near her house. The night was a vivid, picturesque, holiday scene framed with a hue of frosted windows and reflections of red and green decorations glowing in the night. The silvery beams of moonlight from the clear sky above reflected through my car windows. I remember the coldness of her skin when we embraced and the softness of her voice when we wished each other a "Merry Christmas." Life was a world of joy, and Christmas was special like in words of lore. Although I had nothing, I had everything. I knew then I was going to love Jan my whole life. She was the unique moment in my life. I was not prepared for what was happening.

There was a popular Christmas song that season by a doo wop group called The Uniques. The title of the song was *Merry Christmas Darling (1963)*. The lyrics were as if the wordsmith was sitting in the back seat of my '55 Chevy that night taking notes.

He wrote, *Merry Christmas Darling and a Happy New Year, too. I'm so happy just being here with you.* He was peeking inside my soul.

That Christmas vacation, I also received a telephone call from the coaching staff of Northeast Louisiana University. They would be in town the next day if I wanted to sign an athletic scholarship to attend the university. The next night, they arrived at our small two bedroom house. My mother and father greeted them at the door. They came into the house, sat down with us, and told us about NLU. They left out the part about the pretty Chinese girl. I could see the pride in my parents' faces as they talked with the two coaches. For all they had sacrificed for me, I could finally express my love, appreciation, and respect for them.

Returning to school after Christmas vacation, I listened to John Lennon on the radio of my '55 Chevy, singing *Listen, Do You Want to Know a Secret?* I had a secret in my heart that no one knew, except me and John Lennon. He was singing advice through the airwaves as if we were close friends. I couldn't wait to see Jan and tell her.

Jan became a necessity of my life. My list of life's needs became Jan, food, clothing, shelter, air, and water. Jan was at the top of the list. I could do without the others. All of my future plans involved her, high school graduation, college, marriage, happiness, family, and eternity. For the remainder of the high school year, we were inseparable. We were an attractive couple, but I had nothing to do with it. She was the decorated doughnut; I was the hole in the center.

I had two struggles I debated with over and over. I had to win and maintain the respect of her family, and I wasn't sure how. The more difficult of the two struggles was how to have an appropriate relationship with Jan. I wanted Jan to know my love for her was a complete love, not just a desirous physical obsession. I was satisfied with hugging and kissing, because I didn't want to be careless with her affection. Our romance was rapidly being fashioned in the style of a Robert Browning poem.

I was excited about graduation night, but more excited about being with Jan on this special occasion. Her presence far exceeded the event. This was the last gathering of our class, a one-of-a-kind group. These very special people in my life were more than classmates and friends. We all shared a bond of exclusive mutual affection that has made me remember and care for them throughout my lifetime. I am happy when I hear good things about their lives and I am saddened by their misfortunes.

Jan was astounding in her graduation cap and gown. I had rather it been a wedding gown. Her divine countenance was branded in my mind. My feelings for her that night were at an all-time high. I dreamed of waking up the next morning beside her. Our closeness grew as the night wore on and thinking about the closing scene was a struggle between desire and righteousness. Desire was way ahead. The passing hours made Jan an enchantress with command of my every human emotion. Not knowing how or why, but that night I didn't chose celibacy, but celibacy somehow chose me. Why?

We talked incessantly and planned to attend the same college. At a school assembly honoring seniors, we both had earned scholarships to the same university. I was blissfully optimistic and very happy.

When the fall semester of college arrived, however, Jan did not attend. Through her mother's business school connections, she took a job with a promising future with a new company that was located in the city. More disappointing than the job was a rumor that I heard. Her mother did not want her daughter to be around me anymore. I didn't know if it was true or not, but I was conditioned to believe all bad news.

Returning were those old feelings of rejection and unworthiness. Again, I was not good enough, unacceptable. All that I disliked growing up was returning again. I learned not to expect approval but to expect criticism and ridicule.

I was trying to be responsible, but it was bringing disastrous results. Any popularity that I acquired was because of sports. What about me? I was a football fashion in the fall, out of style by the spring, and hanging alone on a clothes rack in a Goodwill Store by the summer.

Chapter 23

A Fun and Disastrous First Semester

Off to college I went with two of my friends, Jack and Don, and my DA Diploma (Dumb Ass) from high school. I pursued a major called "Undeclared" and a minor in "Shooting Pool." Jack, Don, and I had a fun first semester and our grades proved it. I was lonely for Jan, the only girl that could mend my grieving heart. College was different and fun, yet I held out hope that Jan would be there to join me for the spring semester. There were plenty of pretty coeds, but I was only interested in the one not there. No pretty co-ed could replace Jan.

Football remained fun and kept my thoughts away from home for a while. Coach Dixie White was in his first year and was revamping the program. The early workouts were hard, and some players departed in the night. On the field practices were designed like most other schools. As the season got off to a disappointing start, Coach White took his fury out on the team.

He wanted to test the first team offense and defense at practice, so he prepared a scrimmage on a Wednesday night at the stadium. The atmosphere was intense. The starters made up one team, and the non-starters comprised the other. Unfortunately, for all of us non-starters, we would get the best the first team had to offer. As a player for the non-starters, I had a chance to show my ability against our best players.

My play was called in the huddle, and I ripped off a nice run of about eight yards. Coach White lost his composure and began to berate the first team defense. He used every word and more that applied to females in describing their effort, but the words that hurt me the most were when he said, "Run it again." Those words not only hurt my ears but later my face. We were going to run the same play at the defense, and they were in redemption mode. I looked around for a replacement, but no one stepped forward. I knew the play was going to be a disaster this time, but as we were taught, "Just suck it up."

We ran the same misdirection play left, and I received the ball going right between the defensive tackle and the defensive end. The play didn't fool anyone this time. Our returning All-Conference defensive end didn't respond like the girl Coach White said he was. I saw him crashing down in the gap between the tackle and the tight end as I received the hand-off. I saw no place to run except into the belly of the beast. As contact was made, I saw the stadium lights go out and I took a football nap on the field.

When I opened my eyes, the trainer, Coach Martin, was standing over me holding up two or four fingers. I learned from being knocked out before that if you count the fingers and divided by two, you will probably be right. He said I was going to need stitches. I got up and touched my face from under my face mask. My mouth piece was missing, and I felt a large swelling of my lips and some split open flesh. My hand was masked with blood. I walked toward the training room to clean up and get stitched back together. The defense was celebrating their road kill, and Preston, the defensive end, said, "You won't be hugging and kissing for a long time, freshman." Not to be outdone, I smiled through my cracked bloody face and said, "I don't like foreplay anyway; it's a waste of time." An old football axiom is never let them know it hurts. Another is, just because there is blood doesn't mean there is foul play. I don't even know if he understood the bloody bubbly words that came from my flapping, balloon-sized lips, but Coach Martin laughed (probably out of pity).

Football was still fun, and I was receiving some recognition from the coaches. Whenever they needed a human sacrifice for a play, they would show me some love and put me in. Once, I had a very good practice, and the first team defense got mad and wanted to punish me. They threatened me by designating me "bottle material." This meant a group of players would come to your dorm room, strip you naked, spread your butt cheeks open as wide as possible, and spray an aerosol can of petrolatum-based analgesic as far up your rectum as it would go. The fire would burn for days. I decided to keep my dorm room locked for the remainder of the season, and I never answered the door. I think they call it camaraderie.

Near the end of the fall semester, Jack sustained a severe knee injury during football practice. He was going to have surgery done back home at the end of the semester. He decided to recover and rehabilitate his knee at home; therefore, he would not return for the spring. Don had decided earlier during the semester that college wasn't for him. Even though he was doing very well in football, he was not doing very well in class. He just stopped going. No Jack, no Don, no Jan.

At NLU all alone
My friends and love all back home
A careful decision I had to make
My resolution was a mistake
Johnny-Giovanni

To drop out of school, I had to make an appointment with the Dean of Education and the Head Football Coach. I had no intention of telling them why I was leaving, so I had to resort to lying. I couldn't use the financial excuse because I was on a full athletic scholarship. Everything was paid for, room and board, books, laundry allowance, and a monthly stipend. My living accommodations were better than those I grew up with back home. My dorm suite had central heat and air, my roommate had a television set, the bathroom had two separate lavatories, and our room had two separate built in desks with plenty of storage. I liked my roommate, who was also my teammate, a defensive tackle from Baton Rouge. Football was going great. I just turned eighteen in September, and this was only January. I was still a young freshman with a chance to fulfill my dream. I was going to have to think up a believable lie. I didn't want to lie, but I couldn't tell the truth. Was my nose going to grow anymore for lying? No, it was already at maximum length, thanks to my Roman genes. Damn Romans. My lie was going to be that the courses were too hard. I had to study a lot, but I also knew that I could pass.

Expecting a handshake and a good-bye, I met with the Dean. The Dean grilled me like I was a murder suspect. He did not believe the lie that the courses were too difficult. Like looking into a crystal ball, he said, "Is this about some girl back home?" Had he heard this story before, or was I just a bad liar? The Dean finished, "You seem like a nice young man, and if this is about a girl, you can find a new pretty one here. You are making a mistake that will affect the rest of your life." Nevertheless, he signed my release, and I was off to see Coach White.

Coach White's secretary walked me back to his office. Wishing I wasn't there, I sat across from him. Coach was a tough guy who had played in the offensive line at Texas Tech University. He had a large scar across the top of his lip, and when he became angry, the top of that scar would curl up. He was an assistant coach at LSU before accepting the head coaching job at NLU. Most players were intimidated by Coach White, but we believed in him.

I didn't think my news of leaving would matter to him, but I was wrong. There were some players who just left school without telling anyone or officially dropping out. I told Coach White my reason for being there and my excuse for dropping out. His lip began to curl. He showed me the depth chart. I was the number three running back going into spring practice, a big jump from my previous number seven status in September. The previous number one running back was a graduating senior, one had left school, another was moved to a new position, and I assume I had passed someone, but I didn't know it. I had learned in football that if you worked hard and stayed the course, you would eventually get to play. I was only four months into my eighteenth birthday, and now I was leaving. Coach White said, "This is not about some girl back home, is it?" How did he know? Did I look that sad? Coach said he hoped that I would change my mind.

Part Four

Answers 40-42

40. Who was the gunman that shot and killed Lee Harvey Oswald?
    A) Bar owner Jack Ruby
    Jack Ruby stated to the Warren Commission that he shot Lee Harvey Oswald so Jackie Kennedy would not have to return to Dallas for the murder trial of her husband.

41. How many United States Presidents have been assassinated while in office?
    C) Four
    James Garfield, July 2, 1881 (died September 19)
    Abraham Lincoln, April 14, 1865
    William McKinley, September 6, 1901 (died September 14)
    John F. Kennedy, November 22, 1963
    Also, Ronald Reagan was shot on March 3, 1981, and survived. Theodore Roosevelt was shot while campaigning for a third term as the candidate for the Bull Moose Party on October 14, 1912. He continued campaigning and declared, "You see, it takes more than one bullet to kill a Bull Moose." We need more like Teddy. Roosevelt not Kennedy.

42. Where did the phrase *Yes Virginia, There is a Santa Claus* come from?
    B) An editorial by reporter Francis Church in the *New York Sun* newspaper in 1897. Eight-year old Virginia O'Hanlon asked her father, Dr. Philip O'Hanlon, if Santa Claus really existed, He told Virginia that if it's in the *The New York Sun,* then it is so. Dr. O'Hanlon contacted editorial writer Francis Church and he wrote the now famous article.

Part Five

The Wander Years

Chapter 24

Trying to Fall Out of Love

The stairs still lead from the sidewalk
To the house no longer there
Tragedy, friendship and love
Now reside elsewhere
I was seventeen
Concealing my sanguine dream
Of unbroken endless time
Johnny-Giovanni

Leaving behind college life and the game that had been so good to me, I went home. Although the chances were slim, I had to find Jan. I would do anything for her affection. I was hoping for something that wasn't going to happen, still pretending I had a chance.

I went around town seeking employment. One of my stops was at the company where Jan worked. Many of my high school classmates were working for this new company, which eventually became the largest employer in the city. The possibility of working with Jan was the opportunity I sought. I was never hired and could not understand why. Was it chance, was someone else involved, or was someone looking out for me, and I didn't realize it.

I was out one night and met a high school friend for a beer. We were reminiscing about the good times in high school, and then he said the words that still linger today. "You're old girlfriend is getting married." I feigned the words had no effect, but beneath my clothes I felt my body tremble. Jan was about to wed another. The mosaic of dreams that I had designed were shattered. Not an image survived. My voice broke, and then my heart. I quickly walked away. Edgar Alan Poe, not Robert Browning, had written the end to this love story.

I was a recovering Janaholic for many years and continue to miss her sometimes even now. I made some wrong choices and hurt some people trying to fill the void she left in my life. Those you love inevitably become memories.

At times, the familiar hurt is resurrected by some unforeseen cue: an old movie, a song, the high school yearbook, or a former classmate. The Beatles sang my life in two songs, *Yesterday* and *Let It Be*. There was something exceptional about Jan. Regardless if the relationship ended well or not, my love for her will always be. Jan is the final image on my Mount Rushmore.

I was trying to stay real through it all. I was still hoping for my special little place in the world and for someone special to share it with. After the demise of Jan became a reality, I again wandered through the Garden of Eden seeking more forbidden fruit.

I began a series of mistakes. Trying to replace that never again feeling, I began a succession of failed social encounters. Most of the young ladies were very reverent, and I was not interested.

A friend trying to be helpful set me up with a very pretty and nice girl. She had a personality that everyone loved except me. To all, she was pretty, funny, and talkative. To me she was pretty, annoying, and noisy. She was the youngest member of her large family and had some married brothers and sisters that didn't want her to be mistreated. She used their security blanket to wield a vicious sword. Thus, I became a circus performer, and she was the ringmaster.

She barked the commands, and to the delight of her family, friends, and circus watchers, I danced like Bozo the clown. Little did she know that Bozo was about to escape from under the big top. Every one of our dates ended in an argument. Although she was very nice, she was also very spoiled.

One night we were invited to a gathering of her friends. Of course they were her friends because my friends wouldn't attend such a charade. Another argument ensued, and I could hear the organ piping the circus theme in the background. I could smell the popcorn, peanuts and cotton candy. I refused to be shot out of the cannon again in front of the gawking crowd. It was time to remove the makeup, be the person I really was, and leave the circus life behind.

I told her I thought we should leave. I really didn't want to make a scene. After getting everyone's attention and sympathy by performance-enhancing tears and purposefully smearing her mascara, she said, "I'm not riding with you. Call me a taxi." Anyone there would have taken her home, but "Call me a taxi" was so Hollywood dramatic.

Foreseeing that our time together was about to delightfully end, a spirit of peace came over me. Why not acquiesce to one last request? This would have been the perfect time to quote Clark Gable in *Gone with the Wind* but I didn't. I looked at her with a smile and said, "You want ME to call YOU a taxi?" Pretending to be a broken woman, she nodded her head yes. Her friends gathered round to console her. It was easier for her to break up with me than break up with her own ego. With the audience watching, I paused a moment for full effect and when the timing was just right I calmly said, "Okay, you're a taxi!" I walked away happily to a rousing chorus of insults and profanities which I took as applause. Love can only be replaced by a greater love, and she only had love for herself.

43. What is the title of the circus theme song?
   A) *Entry of the Gladiators*
   B) *Here Come the Clowns*
   C) *A Day at the Circus*

The parade of imposters continued with yet another set-up date. This paramour impersonator actually won me over in the beginning. I was not only a dumb ass; I was a naive dumb ass. She paid for the dates, she bought me gifts, we rode in her car, and I believed every untruth she spoke. I developed a fondness for her because I thought she cared for me as a person.

Since she was so good to me, I was going to return the favor with a surprise visit and an appreciative gift. I drove into the parking lot of her apartment, and I saw her. She was dressed for the evening, looking enticing and merry, hand-in-hand with another man. Should I run over them or just drive away? That's how frustrated I had become with women. They drove off to a night of gaiety and fun, and I drove off with a cold beer. I drove around, privately battling my insecurities, flaws, and doubts in the dimming light of the evening.

One Saturday morning, I decided to drive to a nearby lake recreation area to look at the sights and get some rest and relaxation. Trying to be noticed, I strolled along the water's edge with my cool shades, swim trunks, no shirt, and my St. Louis Cardinal Baseball cap.

I was sloshing through the shallow water when I saw a girl that was displaying a look-at-me moment. She was sitting by the water, her lean toned body leaning back on her elbows with her long tan legs resting in the water. She wore an orange one piece swimsuit cut high at the hip and low in the front. Her makeup was perfect, and her brown hair was thick and long. I was expecting her to get up and walk on water across the lake.

She was sounding the dog whistle, and I was running on all fours trying to get there first. As I walked by, I stopped, pretending to view the area. She initiated the conversation with, "Are you looking for anyone in particular?" I took a chance and said, "Not anymore. I think I just found her." She smiled and asked me to sit. Heck, I would even roll over and beg if that would help. We both engaged in a phony conversation, and she was making the moves of a chess master. She asked me if I would rub some tanning lotion on her back. I kindly told her that I would try but I should inform her I was dyslexic. There was a possibility that I might get her front and back mixed-up. She laughed, but she didn't tell me to stop.

She said the afternoon sun was too hot, and she was heading home. She put some towels and lotions in her beach bag and got up from the sand. I took the beach bag from her hand, and put it in my mouth, and walked on all fours to her car. She smiled, probably thinking, "Good dog." She sat in her car and talked to me through the open window. She invited me to stop by her house later that night. She drew a map to her house on a bank deposit slip that also had her address and telephone number. There was no need for a map, I would just follow her scent. She explained that she lived in a rural area off the main road, and it could be difficult to find. Not for me, this canine was already on her trail. It sounded like dog heaven.

She was a nice girl, very pretty, but my only interest was I had nothing else to do. She was the best option for the night. With still some light of day, I called the telephone number on the bank deposit slip. She answered, and I warned her I was about to come over if she wanted not to be home. I think she just wanted some company like I did. She said she lived in a small complex of four mobile homes, and hers was the first one on the right.

With my keen canine instincts, I followed the directions on the map and drove off the main highway onto a dirt road. I saw the small mobile home complex ahead and looked for the house on the right. As I approached, a pack of dogs from the surrounding woods and from under all four mobile homes aggressively converged on my vehicle. They were barking, growling, and snarling in the dust of the dirt road while they circled my car. I parked under a tree near the house, and a black cat jumped from the tree onto the hood of my car. I was more afraid of the dogs than the cat was. My new friend walked out of the doorway of her house and stood on a small front porch. I looked at her for help. The dogs were blocking me from exiting my car, and she tried to call them off with no success.

An older man came out from another mobile home and began chasing the dogs away. It was like a scene from *Deliverance*. If banjo music started playing, I was leaving. The old man was her grandfather, and the other mobile homes were occupied by various relatives. It was a family complex. Everything about me was out of place, my car, the way I was dressed, and my reason for being there. Was this another snafu of my life? Children started riding bicycles and playing. Little girls showed me their dolls and told me their names. People unfolded lawn chairs and sat outside. They explained to me their family tree and shared cobbler recipes. Was I unknowingly the guest of honor for some rural ritual? Was I in danger? No, not at all. They were gracious people showing their hospitality.

I had fun, and by the time I left, I had an assortment of home-grown vegetables, jarred fruits, and an invitation to "come back soon." The evening was nothing like I had anticipated. I was expecting alone time with a high maintenance diva, but this was much better. There are a lot of ways to have a good time, and I just discovered another one. Although this date was one and done, I called her once more and told her of the fun I had had with her family. That was the last time I talked to her. I have a fervent hope that she found a kind man to fulfill her life, one that must love dogs and large family gatherings.

44. Where did the acronym SNAFU originate?
   A) World War II
   B) Civil Rights Movement
   C) U.S. Space Program

Chapter 25

Little Boy Air Force Blue

One day, Jack visited me at my parents' house. He had gone back to NLU after his knee rehab and wanted me to return. I had been out of school for almost a year and had left piles of man poop at every failure along the way. The advice sounded right, but my military obligation was still on my mind. Although my draft eligible number of 342 was far down the list and I was probably safe, I wanted to have a plan even if I returned to school. Jack's knee surgery had classified him as unfit for military service.

I grew tired of living in the past lane and I decided to join the United States Air Force Reserve. Six weeks of basic training and tech school, one weekend a month, two weeks of camp each summer, a chance for regular enlistment if I wanted, and a possible call-up if needed. It was the proper decision for the disorderly time I was trying to navigate. No more dead-end jobs, no more Jan, no more looking for happiness. It would also give Jesus Christ a break from listening to my ridiculous and unworthy appeals.

There was no celebration the night before I left for basic training. I wasn't going to have one last screw-up to remind me of the past. On a cool late November morning, I left for the airport and boarded a flight to Lackland Air Force Base, San Antonio, Texas, for basic training. It was my first flight ever, and I was impressed with the free peanuts and the flight attendants in that order. It was the first time in a while that a woman spoke to me with kindness and truth, even if it was, "Would you like some more peanuts?" We were told not to bring any clothes, except what we would wear on the flight.

When we arrived, a blue USAF bus picked us up for the drive to the military base. We were processed in and taken to the mess hall for a meal. After completing the meal, we went straight to the barracks and went to bed for the night.

The next morning at 5 A.M. the door was pushed open with force, and a booming voice was yelling, "Get your lowlife asses up, it's five o'clock. Do you think you're going to sleep all day?" He continued, "I'm Sgt. Johnson, and you're going to wish you had never met me." I already did. We marched to the mess hall again for breakfast, then went to the supply building to get our clothes and bedding. We changed into our fatigues and had our first lessons on how to make a bed, hang clothes, and roll socks and underwear. The rest of the day was spent on how to clean the barracks and the latrine. We also received the security roster for the remainder of the week. The barracks were to be secured twenty-four hours a day in shifts of four hours each.

The physical part of training was easy, having experienced football practices that were much more strenuous. The other part of basic training was a test of one's mental strength. They tried to create stress to test your character. Whatever the task may be, Sgt. Johnson would always proclaim us to be a "bunch of incompetent, uncoordinated dip shits."

After dinner on the first night of training, some recruits were losing the mental battle, and Sgt. Johnson helped them with his bedtime story. "When you lay down tonight and can't go to sleep, remember your girlfriends are back home cheating on you." In some cases, I knew he was right. For once, I was glad I didn't have a girlfriend. As the lights went out at 8 P.M. and *Taps* played, I heard a few whimpers from those who had girlfriends back home.

As training continued, Sgt. Johnson was prophetic is his use of the words "incompetent" and "uncoordinated." A lot of the trainees were not in shape and were lacking in agility. Other than completing basic training, I remember two episodes vividly in my mind.

One was at the rifle range. On that specific day of training, we were issued M-16 rifles, (I'm sorry, Sgt. Johnson, M-16 weapons). In class, we were taught how to dismantle and clean them, how to load the magazine, and to understand the different settings for firing the weapons automatically and semi-automatically. We proceeded to the firing range for positioning practice. We had to fire from lying down, on one knee, standing upright, and the sitting position. Each trainee was given a target and instructed to load twenty-five rounds in the magazine. Our first firing position was lying down. The instructor would order, "Ready on the right, ready on the left, ready on the firing range." Then, "Ready, aim, fire!" After we finished firing the rounds, he would command, "Cease fire! Cease fire! Put your weapons down!" We would walk to pick up our targets and count the number of hits to see if we qualified for that firing position. Firing only twenty-five rounds, I had twenty-nine holes in my target. I was a marksman plus for hitting the target twenty-nine times with twenty-five shots, and some other trainee was an "incompetent, uncoordinated dip shit" for shooting my target. I was a natural soldier.

The obstacle course seemed to be the most difficult for most troops. You had to complete the course in a prescribed time. The course had hazards, such as climbing a wall, crawling through a simulated mine field, a swinging rope across a pool of water, and some others I can't recall, except for one.

There was a standard of monkey bars about ten feet off the ground that covered a distance of about fifty feet with a muddy body of water below. The technique was simple: alternate hands across the monkey bar rungs until you reached the other side. It required some upper body strength, especially in the arms and shoulders. An instructor would start a trainee, and when the trainee was about half way across, he would start another.

I was moving well across the obstacle when the trainee in front of me stopped a little past half way. As I approached him, I yelled for him to move. He didn't respond so I grabbed the outer supports of the monkey bars and made my way around him (How about that move, Sgt. Johnson). When I passed him, I grabbed the rungs of the bars and continued on my way. I stopped and looked at the hanging troop behind me and said, "Come on. You can make it." He began to maneuver across the bars, and I momentarily waited for him to catch up. Then the unexpected happened. He began to lose his grip and jumped toward me, grabbing me around the waist. I tried to finish the obstacle with him hanging on, but his weight pulled us into the muddy water. I was ashamed of my failure. Sgt. Johnson was right. I was an "incompetent, uncoordinated dip shit."

The barrack inspections were laughable. The inspection crew

would come, and everyone would stand at attention at the side of his bunk. One inspector would put on a pair of white gloves and order the lights to be turned off. He would take out a flashlight and then lie on the floor looking for dust. Then he would move his hand laced with the white glove across the floor and throw a tantrum because the glove would have small particles of dirt on it. Another inspector would walk by each bunk and turn the mattress over onto the floor. All clothing on hangers had to be buttoned completely, and the open end of the hanger was required to be on the back of the hanging rod one inch apart from each hanger. If not, the inspectors would throw all of the clothes on the floor. They would look in your footlocker and check your toothpaste. When used, the tube had to be rolled from the bottom, and no toothpaste was allowed in the cap. Soap had to be dried and shined. All items were required to be in an assigned location with the label facing upward. If not, the inspector would turn over the foot locker.

When they finished the inspection, we had to start over again, because the barracks was ransacked. Men had to be mentally tough and emotionally balanced to handle the sarcasm, profanity, and possible failure of an inspection or obstacle. It was part of the mental game. They were always going to find something wrong and try to break you emotionally. One trainee had tears running down his face, and Sgt. Johnson let loose with, "You incompetent, uncoordinated milksop, crybaby dip shit." It was the first and last time I have ever heard the word "milksop."

The threat of basic training was the evaluation at the end of the week. If you failed the week, you were set back and had to repeat the instructions that had been taught. It was more of a threat than reality, because I knew of no one that had to repeat.

After the six-week recreational holiday of basic training, I was off to technical school at Amarillo Air Force Base, Amarillo, Texas. The school was to teach you how to operate a warehouse, store supplies, locate supplies, issue supplies, handle hazardous materials and explosives, and for some, how to steal supplies and sell them for extra money. The instructors were all amateur comedians with their array of centuries' old military jokes. It was smart to laugh at the jokes, regardless, because the more you laughed, the less instruction you received from the staff mentor.

Tech school was more fun than basic training, because on weekends we could go to the NCO Club for a burger and a beer and watch sports on television. There was always a WAF (Women's Air Force) or two in the club being pursued by the fifty or more tech school students and instructors.

Rather than join the competition for the two WAFs, I would sit and contemplate the situation I had left behind and try to analyze why I was unsuccessful with Jan. I had common sense, but around a beautiful girl, I had no sense whatsoever. The past may have been over, but it lived in me like a dormant emotion that could set me back at any time. Attractive girls with dark hair brought back the memory of only one and could interrupt my thoughts and seize my mind for indefinite amounts of time. I was both eager and frightful of going home. I wanted to exorcise the past from my life.

After graduating from tech school, I was to complete my six months of training at Barksdale Air Force Base in Bossier City, Louisiana. Bossier City was across the Red River from my home. Working at the base was fun, and I enjoyed the military life. When my time was up, I had an exit interview. The CO asked me my plans, and I told him I was going back to college to complete my degree. During my first semester at NLU, I had taken ROTC. The commanding officer said to continue with ROTC, and he would recommend me for officer candidate school. He explained the benefits of being a career military officer. Many times later I wished I had taken his offer. My cousin is a retired Colonel in the United States Air Force. At family gatherings, I have talked with him and learned of his assignment as an exchange pilot with the Royal Air Force and conducting business in the Kremlin in Moscow. He also has had multiple assignments at the Pentagon in Washington, D.C. He is now headmaster at a military prep school in Virginia. The military provided him with a secure and rewarding life.

Chapter 26
NLU Again

I had a good opportunity before me, but I followed the desire in my soul to become a teacher and a football coach. Now, it was back to NLU with my friend, Jack. Friends and family advised me to take something worthwhile, not education and coaching. In a monetary sense, they were correct. I had two loves in life, Jan and football, and I had already lost one. I was not going to lose the other. I didn't plan on a wife or family anymore, so the salary would only be for me. I would be able to work outside with the greatest fraternity of workers, coaches; with the best students to be around, football players; and have the opportunity to win again and again against those schools that I still held grudges against. No other job could provide the satisfaction and elation of being a coach. In my narrow, athletic mind, I would be overpaid.

My second time at NLU was much better. Jack and I rented a house one block from campus with two other friends. We lived like family. We met some fascinating new friends who provided us with good times, fun, and laughter. College life was terrific, except for one area. I had no feelings for the beautiful coeds that walked the campus each day. They had eye appeal but no sex appeal to me.

Throughout our high school years and until then in college, I had never seen Jack show much serious attention toward the ladies. We talked about the campus hotties, some young female instructors, and the girls from high school, but it was just idle men's talk. Jack probably had a few dalliances but wanted to keep them secret. He had that "I'm different; I don't need anyone" image to uphold. Nevertheless, after an NLU football game one Saturday night, we made the rounds to the various parties. It was the first time I had ever seen Jack show any interest in a girl. Of course, she was not a normal girl.

Rosemary (real name) had long kinky hair, a bespectacled face, a headband, and many rings and bracelets, even a very sexy one on her ankle. Her style and swagger were more attractive than her physical appearance. She was as unconventional as Jack. I saw that Jack was interested in Rosemary, so I left the party and headed back to the house. Jack returned later that night in love with Rosemary. Sunday evening he invited Rosemary to the house.

Jack was going to grill some burgers, and I would get to meet the first girl ever to steal his heart. Rosemary arrived later that day, and she looked much more attractive in the daylight than at the party. Beneath that altered look of rebellion was a pretty young lady.

We began to chat with the usual college talk of what's your major and where are you from. Rosemary said her major was pharmacy. I thought, "She had a good brain along with her unconventional beauty." I asked her, "Why pharmacy?" I expected the usual response of "It pays well, and it's a good career. "But this was Rosemary. Her answer was, "I don't want to become a pharmacist. I just like drugs." Bewildered by her answer and trying to be discreet, I got up to walk away. I knew I was overmatched. The only drug I had taken was Janacillin back in high school. The side effects were terrible. It left me feeling depressed. She shouted, "Morphine is my favorite drug, what's yours?" Trying to sound-drug informed, I said, "I had ecstasy in high school." Surely, she would think I was talking about the drug and not a girl. Rosemary was a temptress. I could see myself walking on the wild side hand in hand with Rosemary. She had a seductive allure that made me interested, but I knew to walk away. I bid Rosemary a safe "trip" and whispered to Jack, "Please be careful. You don't need a real Rosemary's baby."

45. What actress starred in the 1968 psychological horror film *Rosemary's Baby*?
    A) Mia Farrow
    B) Ali McGraw
    C) Meryl Streep

I learned how to study and was a more dedicated student this time around. I was making the Dean's List consistently. My grades were much better than they were in high school. I enjoyed learning and I still do today. Education gave me confidence in myself and the encouragement to write this book. Once I made the Dean's List, I wanted to make it every semester. My study sessions became longer and more intense. Economics was one of my most challenging courses. Going into the final exam, I had an "A," but I had to make an "A" on the exam to maintain it. The questions were not a problem, but Professor Norris always had an analysis problem where a graph had to be constructed, and a conclusion had to be determined. I was concerned, but earning a "B" in Economics was all I had been hoping for since the beginning of the course.

I sat at the first seat on the first row by the door for the exam. Professor Norris would pass out the test by hand, giving each student a test paper. He started the procedure with me, so I received the first test from the stack. There were fifty test items on the page. As I examined the paper closely, I could detect the answers imprinted on each item. Professor Norris must have made the answer key on the first paper, and the imprint of the answers came through on the second paper, which was the one I received.

He placed the stack of page one test papers on his desk and pick up another stack of papers, which were page two. He distributed page two of the test, I examined my copy closely, and the same thing happened. Thus, I had the answers to the entire test. Should I or shouldn't I was the decision. Without hesitation, I went up to Professor Norris and showed him his mistake. He wrote my name on the two papers, placed the grade "A" on the test, and told me I was excused. Honesty IS the best policy. When I was teaching in high school, I considered using this procedure to test the honesty of specific students. I never did because I didn't want to risk the chance of being disappointed in anyone.

There was another particular happening in a class when a classmate saved me from ignorance. I was enrolled in an elective course entitled Music Appreciation. I enjoyed the class enormously, and the instructor was first-class. We learned the names and sounds of different instruments, different styles of classical music, and biographies of composers and their works. We were assigned operas and classical music to review from the music library. The tests in class were fun. The professor would play the sound of an instrument, and we would have to identify it, or he would play a piece of classical music, and we had to distinguish the style or recognize the composer. He even taught us some musical notes, and we had to compose a short musical composition. I was impressed at how he captured my interest about a topic I thought was irrelevant to my existence.

One day in class he was lecturing about composer Wilhelm Richard Wagner of Germany. There is a music festival every year in Germany honoring him. He was using the German pronunciation of his name; therefore, he kept saying "Vogner." He told the class to find the pages on "Vogner" in our text. I checked the index under the letter "V" for Vogner and couldn't find it. I looked around the room to insure that I had the same text book as the other students. I went through the alphabet writing the last letters on my paper, "U, V, W, X. Y, and Z." I was searching the correct letter, "V," but I couldn't locate the word Vogner.

As he continued his lecture, I began to panic. He was identifying things in the text and I couldn't find the page. The other students, mostly music majors, were underlining and highlighting things the professor was emphasizing. I concluded that my text book was a misprint. I was about to raise my hand and say my book didn't have the section about "Vogner." As I was about to put my hand in the air, a diminutive stereotypical nerd sitting next to me grabbed my arm, pointed to the page in his book, and highlighted the name "Wagner." I was rescued from assdom by my new BFF. If he would have let me commit scholastic suicide, I would have never returned to that class. I would have dropped the course and arranged for plastic surgery. I bid a toast of gratitude from me to the music nerds all over the world. I now watch the marching band perform at half time of football games and think of my BFF.

Another close encounter with stupidity took place in the microbiology lab. Jack and I were in the same class from 4-5 P.M. on Thursdays. The instructions for our final exam were to take a Petri dish with agar, take a needle from one of five jars of bacteria, rub it across the agar, cover the Petri dish, and let it stand for twenty-four hours. After twenty-four hours we were to go back into the lab and run a series of tests to determine what type of bacteria was growing. The lab instructor warned us to use sterile techniques, because if we didn't, we might have more than one growth, and it would be impossible to identify which growth was the test sample.

Most of the students in the lab were pharmacy students and had no problems. Jack and I went back the next day to check on our Petri dishes. We both had so many different types of growth they spilled over the side of the Petri dish and pushed the top of the Petri dish up on one side. It looked like we were going to have to repeat microbiology lab or run our tests on one of the many growths and hope that was the one from the jar. The lab assistant was a graduate student, and she recognized our dilemma. She knew that we were not pharmacy students and had sympathy for us. She checked the log for what type of bacteria we were supposed to have. She prepared our Petri dish agar with sterile procedures and told us the name of our bacteria. We returned the next day, checked our Petri dish, wrote our findings on the lab sheet, turned it in, gave the lab assistant a hug, and talked about changing our majors to pre-med.

Chapter 27

A Degree in Sanitation and Humility

As the spring semester ended, I needed to find a summer job back home to help finance my college tuition. I didn't know anyone influential, so I was on my own. One of my high school friends from the past was in town for the summer, also. He told me he had heard the city Sanitation Department paid regular wages, not minimum wage, for summer workers.

I drove down to the city incinerator, parked among the almost disabled vehicles in the lot, and walked toward the office. As I passed the incinerator, I could hear the excitement of thousands of flies blanketing the piles of garbage. As more garbage was dumped, they would fly about in innumerable directions and seemed to land in unison on the fresh garbage. Their performance was captivating. I wanted to meet the fly who choreographed this show. This was the beginning of my relationship with the *musca domestica*, or the common housefly. They lay their eggs in garbage. The eggs appear as small grains of rice. They hatch within twenty-four hours, and housefly larvae, or maggots, emerge.

There was no interview process, no orientation, no physical, and no chance to back out. I started working immediately on the same Monday I arrived.

The turnover rate was high. One new worker on my truck that day quit within fifteen minutes. He went behind a house to dump the owner's twenty-five gallon garbage can into his forty-gallon issued can and never returned to the truck. The driver asked me to go check on him. I found his empty issued can in the backyard, but he had vanished. We would have had to finish our route that day with only two collectors, but the driver helped us out. Each driver had a can in case of an emergency, and this was an emergency. The driver knew that if he didn't help, we might also quit, and he might have to complete the route all alone. More than half of the new workers didn't report for work by the second day.

In the 1960s, there were no compactor trucks and city-issued home garbage containers as there are today. Each collector was issued a metal forty-gallon receptacle. Homeowners were not required to put their garbage on the street. Most stored their cans on the side or behind their house. A sanitation worker was expected to collect the garbage from two or three houses, walk to the truck, reach up over his head, and dump his container into the back of the trailer truck. Height and strength were an advantage. When the trailer was almost full, we climbed into the trailer and "stomped the garbage down" to compact it to make more room. We went to the dump or the incinerator twice a day, once before lunch and once at the end of the route.

Each crew had two routes. One route was collected on Mondays and Thursdays. The second route was picked up on Tuesdays and Fridays. Wednesdays and Saturdays were trash days. Trash was considered yard clippings, tree limbs, broken furniture, old tires or anything the homeowner wanted to discard. Garbage was the tin cans, bottles, food preparation boxes, or anything from the kitchen.

Mondays and Tuesdays were the most difficult days because a lot of garbage was accumulated over the weekend. After working two summers for the city Sanitation Department, I have a lot of respect today for garbage collectors. I bag all of my garbage myself and make the collection as clean and easy as possible for those workers. As they say, "I've been there and done that."

The next day, Tuesday, I was placed on a four-man truck crew consisting of our driver, Rocky, and garbage men, James, Chuck, and me. We had a crew of four because of the large routes. I was the youngest and the only Caucasian. That's a clever way to say the others were black, not that it's necessary. Rocky, James and Chuck were veterans. I knew that if I worked my hardest and treated the guys with respect, everything would be satisfactory. They knew I was a college student and a summer worker. They accepted me into their world with no indifference. By the end of the summer, we had a mutual respect for each other.

I had difficulty eating lunch after lifting and dumping garbage all morning. What made me that way? There are a FEW reasons. When our truck would stop on a residential street, we would grab our cans and head toward the houses. Mamas, grandmothers, or babysitters would ALWAYS tell the children, "Come in the house now! Here comes the garbage man." Dogs would bark and become angry. No one liked the garbage man. If the homeowner's can was in the back of a fenced yard, someone would come outside and say, "Don't you let my dog out." While you emptied their can into yours, the dogs would snarl, snap, circle, bark, and sometimes bite. Some people would watch to make sure their garbage was emptied entirely. They would call you back if they felt slighted. I opened garbage cans where large rats jumped out, or the deceased family pet would be inside, opened-eyed and waiting to be taken away. Spoiled food would be covered with live maggots, and some always seem to find a home somewhere on your body.

After our morning session, we drove to the dump. The dump, or land fill had fires burning in different locations and a worker on a bulldozer leveling the piles of garbage left behind by the trucks. He was equipped with high boots and a gun strapped to his side as he waded through the filth, debris, and waste. He would shoot and kill any bird, rodent, or scavenger that was trying to steal from the muck.

As the truck stopped, the driver would put into motion a 4 x 8 wooden draw gate that pushed the accumulation of garbage out of the trailer from the cab to the end of the trailer bed onto the ground. Then, we would get up in the trailer to sweep out the remains and place the draw gate back in the trailer. The driver reversed the cable, and the draw gate was pulled back in place against the cab of the truck.

Then, it was off to some convenience store for rest and lunch. I usually wasn't hungry, but I would get something to drink. I would lie down on the grass in the shade with my eyes closed, mentally preparing myself for the hotter afternoon collection. I learned something about myself. I tried just as hard at garbage collecting as I did at any job.

46. Who wrote the 1906 novel *The Jungle* about unsanitary practices in the meat packing industry?
   A) Lincoln Steffens
   B) Upton Sinclair
   C) Jacob Riis

After lunch that day, Tuesday afternoon, we set out to complete our Tuesday-Friday route. We were driving toward an older, more affluent part of town. When the truck came to a halt, I was ready to become a deserter like many of the rest, but not because of the toilsome labor of the job or my garbage man status in the eyes of community. We were one block from Jan's house which she shared with her new husband. Like they say, if not for bad luck, I'd have no luck at all. Her mother had lived there before she moved to another state; therefore, I knew the location. I was about to pick up the garbage of my beloved heart's desire from the recent past. What a way to renew our acquaintance! Should I leave a note on her garbage can?

James and Chuck always let me work the right side of the street where the truck would park, so I wouldn't have to carry my garbage across the street if there was traffic. As we turned right, I could see their residence about five houses away on the right. It was Tuesday afternoon, and I was trying to convince myself through a lot of agony that no one would be home.

The truck parked in front of the third house on the right. James and Chuck crossed the street to the other side. I pulled down my baseball cap, adjusted my sun glasses, took my deep round container, and walked in the direction of house number one. I picked up the garbage from the first three houses and returned to dump the contents into the truck. After I finished, the truck moved forward and stopped in front of the newlywed's home. Trying to hide an unpleasant and worried look on my face, I worked house number four on the block and headed for my "new" encounter with Jan. My rapidly pounding heartbeat was creating panic and anxiety, just as it is now. Their garbage pails were located on the left side of the house. I walked across the front yard and dropped my collection barrel next to their overflowing receptacles. I saw a swimming pool and patio in the backyard. My mind rushed back to a vision of Jan in her two piece swim suit that she had worn on our trip to the lake after our senior year. Carelessly, I tried to empty the cans as quickly as possible, but trash and garbage was falling to the ground. I picked it up by hand. One envelope looked back at me from the ground with her new married name and address on it. It read, Mrs. Happily-Married Jan.

I thought I heard a car and almost lost my urine as I looked to see if anyone was driving down the street, and if so, I begged Jesus not to let it be Jan. Was this the storm on the horizon I would face every Tuesday and Friday? Next time, would Clint Eastwood, or Jan's new husband be standing in the yard, pointing a rifle at me, and saying, "Get off my lawn"? Even though my forty-gallon container was overloaded and heavy, my adrenaline rush allowed me to pick it up with ease. I wanted out of there ASAP. I bypassed our truck and swiftly paced to the next house. I stomped the garbage down in my can, cleaned up house number six, and wobbled with the heavy load to the truck to dump my assortment of garbage. I was ahead of Chuck and James.

Rocky met me at the truck with a smile and said, "Hey, college boy, you must like this job, you tryin' to get put on regular?" Trying not to offend my friends,I answered, "The fringe benefits are like no other." Rocky added, "Shop all day and all you can eat while on the job." The "shop all day" reference was to the many broken items from the trash the workers collected and took home and repaired: furniture items, old bicycles, broken appliances, and discarded toys. Of course, the "all you can eat" referred to the kitchen waste that we hauled away. I guess the garbage without the maggots might have been edible.

It seemed like I could never escape things that would remind me of Jan. What were the odds with all of the houses in the city that her house would be on my garbage route? The coincidences didn't end there.

Another time, I was sent to help teach a Driver's Education class at another school. Jan's daughter was not only in the class, but the instructor teaching the class assigned me as her driving instructor. Even more unlikely was something that happened a few years later. My son came home and told me he had gone out with a girl, and her mother knew me. Yes, the girl was Jan's daughter. Was I trapped in the Twilight Zone?

The garbage men pranks were the worst you could imagine. It was usually played on the driver because he had the easiest job. Jealousy, I presume. Chuck and James would throw a variety of garbage items into the cab of the truck while we were driving to the next location. We would usually hang on to the side of the truck standing on the running boards when we had only a short distance to go. Chuck from one side and James from the other would toss large maggots, used female hygiene items, dead squirrels, dead birds, fish heads, live insects, bird eggs, soiled teddy bears, half-eaten turkey legs, dead cats, feces, or the worst of what garbage had to offer that day. Rocky would retaliate by turning corners fast, trying to make us fall off the truck while we hung precariously on the side, by driving away as we walked up to the truck to dump our drums of garbage, or leaving us at the dump site so we had to ride in the trailer of another garbage truck back to the incinerator.

The garbage trucks would sometimes race each other at the dump to see who the best driver was. In one race, our hood came open, and the battery dislodged from the truck. We had to go back and look for it so we could get home.

Story telling was embellished with more lies than a philandering husband. I will only note one and disavow knowledge of the others. Most were obscene, so I will try to clean this one up as much as possible.

One day at lunch, while leisurely reclining in the grass, the question became what business would you own if you had a choice. Chuck was the first speaker at the impromptu business convention by expressing his desire to own a combination whore house and café. His reasoning was logical. It would be enjoyable, or should I say satisfying, to interview the applicants, and have a good meal after the interview. He backed it up by saying everybody liked a cold beer and something to eat after they make love and before they go home. Of course, he didn't say "make love." He used a more beastly term, but remember, I'm trying to clean up this garbage; that's my job.

One memorable inquiry was if you were rich, what would you buy first? Rocky opened with, I'd buy a yacht boat at least 100 feet long." Chuck asked, "Where would you keep it?" Spoken like a billionaire, Rocky said, "I'd build me a big swimming pool in the backyard and keep it there." Utter brilliance.

Other topics included who was the most famous person that you picked up garbage from; what's the best thing you ever found in garbage; if you could have any garbage route, which one would it be?

Some tall tales were also told. There was a mystery woman who would spray her garbage with expensive perfume, the same kind she wore. They added, "Probably imported from France." Without a doubt.

An old rich man who would leave a Christmas card with a hundred dollar bill in it taped to the lid of his garbage can every holiday season.

There was a story of a nude sunbather in the backyard who never covered up while you were picking up her garbage and showed you everything.

Then there was one about a love-damaged boy who had to pick up the garbage of his lost love and her new husband. That one might be the most unbelievable.

On my last day of work that first summer, James was going to buy me lunch. He knew that I didn't eat lunch while working, and I would refuse any offer. That was the reason he was going to buy me lunch.

We stopped at one of our friendly neighborhood convenience stores, and James bought a pound cake, four slices of baloney, four slices of cheese, and two beers. We went outside, and he sliced the pound cake into bread-like portions. He put some mayonnaise on the pieces of cake and made two double pound cake baloney and cheese sandwiches. He offered me one of the sandwiches and a beer. I told him how much I appreciated the offer, but since I had not eaten lunch all summer, I didn't know how my body would react. James ate both of the sandwiches and drank both of the beers, and we both got our wish.

One day my mother drove me to work because she needed to use my car. As we were leaving the dump that afternoon, I mentioned that I was going to have to call my mother to pick me up at the incinerator because she used my car that day. Rocky said, "No need brother. I'll take you home." We didn't go back to the incinerator as I anticipated. Instead, Rocky drove me home in the garbage truck. I vacated the truck and told him thanks. I've never been driven home by a chauffeur-driven limousine, but I feel safe to say you've never been driven home by a Rocky-driven garbage truck. The conviviality among our crew proved to me that you can't predict mankind.

The title of "most unusual personality" at the Sanitation Department belonged to a man named Travis Manus. He drove the dead animal truck. He had a regulation dump truck equipped with a rotating red light atop the cab and a short wave radio to divulge his location and receive his next call. Attached to the truck were two shovels, a rake, and a pitchfork.

Concerned citizens would call in to the department and report dead animals on the roadway or sidewalk. These could be animals such as dogs, cats, raccoons, opossums, armadillos, or anything large. Travis would drive to the location and load the animal carcass into the back of the dump truck. He would return to the incinerator and dump his gathering of dead animals into the fire. I'm sure there was some type of health code that required they be incinerated.

Our crew was out working one day and Travis drove up beside our truck and said, "I got a call about a dead dog on this street. Have you seen it?" Rocky said, "It was laying up ahead against the curb." Travis drove his truck up to the dead dog, and Rocky drove our garbage truck adjacent to the dead animal truck. Travis got out of the truck eating a sandwich. He wore a Houston Astros baseball cap, a button up shirt that was completely unbuttoned and open, old blue jeans, and leather boots. The conversation that took place in imperfect English went like this.

Rocky: "Where'd you get the baseball hat?"
Travis: "I used to pitch for the Astros."
Rocky: "What happened?"
Travis: "They sent me down."
James: "To pick up dead animals?"
Travis: "That's funny, G-Man"
Chuck: "How did you get this job?"
Travis: "I guess you can say, I love animals."
Rocky: "What's the best dog you ever picked up?"
Travis: "A purdy Collie, looked just like Lassie. He was so purdy that I didn't wanna take him to the incinerator. I took him home and buried him in my back yard. Ain't never run across another one."

Rocky: "You mean nobody else ever ran across another one."
Travis: "Real funny, G-Man."

Travis finished eating his sandwich and wiped his hands along the thighs of his jeans. He nudged the dead dog with his boot.

Chuck: "Why did you do that?"
Travis: "Sometime they still be alive." Pointing to his pant leg, he said, "One grabbed my paints rite cheer one time. Dum ice."
Rocky: "What did you do?"
Travis: "I hit him with my shovel, kilt him again."
Chuck: "I thought you said you were an animal lover?"
Travis: "Real funny, G-Man."

Travis took his wide shovel off the truck and with one swoop tried to sling the dead dog into the back of the truck. The dog fell off the shovel and back into the street. Travis put the shovel down, reached and grabbed the dead dog by the front legs, and hurled it high into the back of the truck. Feeling a sense of accomplishment, he said, "I toll y'all I pitched for the Astros," somehow validating the fact by his dead-animal-tossing skills. He got in his truck and drove away to his next pick up.

I went back a second summer to join my friends, but most had moved on. After graduating from college the next year, I received a call from the department. They had started a GED Adult Education Program for the workers and they wanted me to be the instructor. After work, school was in session from 5 P.M.-7 P.M. I assisted the men with their workbooks and assignments. I was appreciative and proud to serve these hardworking cohorts of my G-Man days. Those kind men definitely influenced my outlook on life.

Part Five

Answers 43-46

43. What is the title of the circus theme song?

A) *Entry of the Gladiators*

Entry of the Gladiators is a military march composed by classical Czech composer Julius Fucik in 1897. The song gained popularity in North America in 1910 when circuses started using it to introduce the clowns.

44. Where did the acronym SNAFU originate?

A) World War II

The word "SNAFU" refers to a bad situation or a mistake. Situation Normal All Fouled Up. Although the origin is questionable, most agree that it began when cynical GI's in World War II ridiculed the military's use of so many acronyms.

45. What actress starred in the 1968 psychological horror film *Rosemary's Baby*?

A) Mia Farrow

Mia Farrow played, Rosemary Woodhouse, whose pregnancy was taken over by her eccentric neighbors. Her husband was cooperating with the neighbors who were part of a cult with sinister plans for her baby. Her baby turned out to be the spawn of Satan.

46. Who wrote the *The Jungle,* about unsanitary practices in the meat packing industry?

B) Upton Sinclair

Sinclair was a journalist and novelist. He had done an investigation into the practices of the meat-packing industry in Chicago. His book contributed to the passage of the Pure Food and Drug Act.

Part Six

Hallowed Halls, Near Collisions, and the Sidelines

Chapter 28

Students, Parents and Head Dudes

I was a member of two great career fraternities: teaching and coaching. While some students avoid teachers entirely, others want to share their life story. One timid, sheepish young girl wanted more than anything to be in the mainstream of high school life. Perhaps she fantasized about a Prince Charming or wanted to impress me with her womanly exploits, thinking I would consider her "high school normal."

One day, the bell sounded for lunch, and the students, as usual, rushed out of the room. She, on the other hand, remained behind as if she had a problem. I started the conversation with, "Aren't you going to lunch?" She put her head down and asked if she could stay in the room. I told her she was not allowed to be in the room alone and would have to go to lunch with the others.

With my lunch time passing quickly, I was trying to get her out of the room. Then I realized that listening to her problem was probably more important than lunch on a Friday. I asked, "All right, tell me what is bothering you." She said her boyfriend wanted her to spend the night with him at his trailer and she didn't know what to do. Obviously, I was not the one to ask for advice about relationships because my scorecard was no wins and all losses. Nevertheless, I gave her the standard counselor talking points; if he really loves you, he will respect you and not force you to do something you might regret; if you are apprehensive now, I don't think it is a good idea; there's no guarantee that it is going to be a special event. I did my best to convince her otherwise but left the decision to her.

The weekend passed, and I never gave her story a thought. Monday arrived, and another week of school began. Again, the lunch bell rang, and I was waiting by the door to exit behind the last running student. I looked back, and there she was sitting at her desk again just like the past Friday. I really didn't want to know the outcome of her weekend tryst. Then she resumed the story from the past Friday. "I spent the weekend with my boyfriend at his trailer," she said. I didn't know what to say, so I just stared at her waiting for the conclusion of the story while thinking about my diminishing lunch time. Then, the lightning bolt from the sky: "I think I'm pregnant." Now, I was mad. This whole story was obviously a hoax. I was about to destroy her with some facts about the birds and bees, but I hesitated and realized I didn't need to humiliate her. (I had some experience in being humiliated, myself.) Giving advice and thinking about the lunch I was missing, I played along with the story.

The remainder of the week passed without a word about the "pregnancy." The following Monday there was a repeat performance. The rest of the class rushed to lunch and she stayed behind at her desk. Hoping she could see the pity in my face and hear the grumbling of my stomach, I looked at her through hunger-pained eyes, but she didn't move. Again, I felt sympathy for the girl and forfeited my lunch time for what I was hoping the final episode of this trilogy. I was ready for the happy ending. I thought, "She had the baby, they got married, and they all will live happily ever after."

With a look of pitiful dejection, she declared, "I got an abortion." Within a span of ten days, this girl slept with her boyfriend for the first time ever, got pregnant, and had an abortion. Within those same ten days, I lost three meals and an hour and half of my life. In reality, mine was the bigger loss, but it was worth it to be a comforting listener to a lonely girl's make-believe world.

In education, they always say you need to make the lesson interesting by trying to make the event "come alive." Our topic was the Exploration of the World, and the explorer for that day was Christopher Columbus. My plan was to present a few facts about Columbus, most of which were in a short film we would watch. I could tell I was making ol' Chris come to life. *He's alive!*

To complete my introduction, I attached a picture of Columbus to the chalk board. I told the class it was his yearbook picture. *He's alive!* Beneath his portrait I wrote born circa. October, 1451, and died May, 1506. I wrote that he was from Italy but sailed for Spain and discovered part of America. I told the class he had made four voyages and that eventually led to the settlement of North America.

I turned out the lights and started the projector. On the screen was a low rent actor in a cheap wig portraying Columbus. (The school board knows how to cut costs.) It appeared buckets of water were thrown from the side of a boat portraying a storm that wasn't there. Somehow, the sailors survived the buckets of water, the fan on high speed, and the simulated storm. The men aboard the *Santa Maria* began to mutiny, but all was forgiven when they saw land. Columbus was triumphant, and his sailors rejoiced in their findings.

I turned on the lights for our concluding discussion. I felt the lesson was educational, and I had brought Columbus to life more so than I thought. I stood in front of the class to begin our discussion, and a young man on the front row raised his hand. I acknowledge him and asked if he had a question or comment. He said, "I thought you said Columbus was dead." *He's alive! He's alive!*

Having no response and avoiding embarrassing the student, I exclaimed, "Thanks for paying attention, end of discussion." Some students never believe the teacher. In our study of Presidents, was I going to have to find Abe Lincoln so he could tell us about his assassination?

I learned so much about the world by teaching geography. I can't make the same claim for my students. To prepare for a lesson, I would construct maps, research topography, and study the history and culture of a region and the significant people of a country. As part of my certification, a Central Office supervisor was to make an official observation of my class and evaluate my instruction. As I should have learned, even thorough preparation doesn't cover all questions.

I was attempting to teach climate zones of the world based on latitude lines and the direct rays of the sun. To begin my presentation, I drew a circle representing the earth. All were familiar with that, except a few. I drew a flat line for the non-believers.

I entered a line at the North Pole and labeled it 90 degrees and a line at the South Pole and labeled it 90 degrees. Everyone seemed to understand. Then, I marked a line across the center of the circle which indicated the equator and numbered it zero degrees. No questions so far. I used a dotted line 23 1/2 degrees north of the equator indicating the Tropic of Cancer and a dotted line 23 1/2 degrees south of the equator indicating the Tropic of Capricorn.

I stood back, admired my illustration, and glanced at the class. In turn, they smiled. Then, I went into the teaching phase, explaining how the direct rays of the sun only shine between the Tropic of Cancer, the equator, and the Tropic of Capricorn. I drew a small circle representing the sun with some squiggly lines portraying the sun rays, and I extended the lines to the equator and the Tropics. To culminate my explanation, I said, "Because the sun's rays only shine directly between the Tropics and the equator, those areas of the world have warm to hot climates year round, and those areas in the far north and south, like the North Pole and South Pole, have cold climates year round because they are farthest from the sun."

Knowing my performance was intelligent and instructive, I asked reluctantly, "Are there any questions?" A pretty little girl on the front row said, "I don't believe you." With my teaching reputation on display in front of the supervisor, I kindly said, "What do you mean?" Feeling certain about her understanding, she conveyed, "Even I know that 90 degrees is hot and zero degrees is cold. You've got it backwards." Then another student agreed, "Yeah, she's right." I looked at the supervisor for help, but she just left the room.

For every successful lesson there are some students that just don't understand. We were studying the Caribbean islands. I showed how some islands were independent and some were owned by other countries. My example was "Cuba is independent, but islands owned by other countries are indicated by the abbreviation of the country that possesses it. Aruba is owned by the Netherlands, indicated by the abbreviation Neth. To check for understanding, I asked, "Find Puerto Rico and tell me what country owns it." An energetic girl was the first to raise her hand and said, "I know! I know!" Admiring my teaching skills,

I asked, "Who owns Puerto Rico?" She said, "We do." I said, 'Very good. That's correct." Then I went one step too far, asking, "And how do you know that?" She told me, "It says 'us' right beside it." Some responses don't need an explanation. This was one.

Some things about the world of education I learned by observing my superiors that I respectfully refer to as the "head dudes." I was assigned front door security at a pep assembly in the gym. It was a hot September afternoon, and the air conditioning system was losing the battle with the heat. The students were singing with the band and chanting death to Friday night's opponent. A girl in the bleachers near the door passed out, and I went inside the gym to assist.

An assistant principal was quickly on the scene and told me to take her out into the foyer of the gym. I gathered her in my arms, walked out of the gym, and gently placed her on the floor. I placed a student's book bag under her head to elevate it and hoped the coolness of foyer air would be enough to resuscitate her. The assistant principal took charge and cried out, "Get the first aid kit! Hurry!" A secretary ran to the office and brought back the white metal box emblazoned with a red cross. He instructed, "Stand back!" Surely he wasn't going to use a defibrillator.

I recalled my first aid training as a coach, and it was to provide immediate and temporary care to the victim of an accident or illness until the services of a professional can be obtained. He was no professional. It meant to keep them still and quiet and call for help, but "head dudes" never let a chance at recognition go by. He removed the book bag from under her head and replaced it with the first aid kit and said, "Go call for help!" The young lady regained consciousness in the open air and began to smile. Removing that book bag and replacing it with the first aid kit probably saved the girl's life. Now I know the proper use of a first aid kit in an emergency. Place it under the victim's head.

People were slapping the assistant principal on the back and shaking his hand proclaiming, "Good job." I agreed. He had done a good job of placing the first aid kit in just the right spot. If not, who knows what could have happened. That is why he is a head dude.

One early morning, I arrived at school and went to the locker room, as usual. Some of the other coaches had arrived, and we were talking. We were all summoned to the principal's office for an emergency meeting. The principal told us someone had called in a bomb threat for the school. Instead of calling the fire department's bomb squad, he assigned each of us an area to cover. His final instruction was, "If you see something suspicious, and it might be a bomb, pick it up and bring it to my office." I wasn't qualified to make the decision, but I was qualified to have an opinion. Mr. Head Dude, no one needs to pick up a potential bomb.

One lunch period, I had restroom duty. I would patrol the restrooms and make sure there was no loitering or illegal activity going on. I walked into one restroom and could see and smell that someone in the last stall was smoking a cigarette. I knocked on the stall door and ask the student to step out. He threw his cigarette in the toilet and stepped out. He was about 4'8"tall, or I should say 4'8" short. He had his cigarette pack in his pants pocket. I took the cigarettes and pretended to read the label. I scolded him; "It says here that the Surgeon General says cigarette smoking may hazardous to your health. He answered with a smart ass, "So?" I don't like to try and reason with unreasonable people. Still pretending to read from the pack of cigarettes I said, "It also says the smoker must be taller than the cigarette, so I guess you're in violation." Off he went to be suspended. All I wanted was a "Yes, sir."

One of my favorite topics to teach was the Constitution of the United States. We were reading the Bill of Rights and listing our constitutional privileges. The First Amendment lists five freedoms: the freedom of speech, freedom of the press, freedom of assembly, freedom of petition, and the freedom of religion.

I was relating how a person can freely attend any church or not participate in religion, if they so desire. I heard a student whisper to another, "I don't like churches." Pouncing on the opportunity, I told him that was his right, but he should not discriminate against those who prefer religion. His puzzled look caught my attention. He said, "Coach, what are you talking about?" I said, "The religious rights of the First Amendment." He answered, "I wasn't talking about the First Amendment, I was talking about chicken. I don't like Church's, I like

Popeye's." So I told him, because of the First Amendment, he had the right to buy chicken anywhere and he should not discriminate against people who buy their chicken at Church's. He said he understood the First Amendment much better now.

47. How many amendments make up the Bill of Rights?
    A) Five
    B) Ten
    C) Fifteen

One time I committed a gaffe in front of the class and tried to squirm my way out of it. I was explaining the Presidential Election of 1912 and the three candidates: Woodrow Wilson, William Howard Taft, and Theodore Roosevelt. Taft and Roosevelt had won previous elections, and I was overusing the word "election" when the word that came from my mouth was the "erection" of 1912. This was the short attention span generation, and I had hoped no one was listening.

Needless to say, I saw a few smiles, snickers, and quizzical looks. Finally, one bold boy said, "Coach, did you say the erection of 1912?" I had to get out of this and save face. I admitted to it and said, "Yes, I was describing Woodrow Wilson's elation when he was told he won the election of 1912." The class roared with laughter. Teachers must have the ability to think quickly. I could be a head dude.

The administration always preferred to assign the incorrigibles to my class. I guess we had something in common. Every November we would have an outside assembly honoring the members of our military on Veteran's Day. The format was usually an introduction of veterans from each branch of the service, military music, a speech, and at the end of the ceremony, a 21-gun salute to honor those deceased veterans. Seven soldiers in uniform would fire three times upon command.

When I received the itinerary for the ceremony, I noticed my class was to stand near the rifle squad. How could the head dudes not see that this was a potential for trouble? Realizing this could be an embarrassing moment for the firing squad and disrupt the solemn service, I tried to educate my class on what was going to take place. I carefully explained the formal dignified right of the occasion and the 21-gun salute at the end of the ceremony was to show respect for our deceased soldiers. I preached, "Do not be alarmed at the 21-gun salute, don't hit the ground, and above all, don't return fire!"

Off we marched to the assembly and took our place near the rifle team. We stood motionless and quiet as the weapons were fired. Most of the crowd was taken by surprise and jumped or screamed. Not my dirty two dozen. Maybe not to you, but to me it was a very proud moment in my career. We did not embarrass or harm the military rifle squad, the ceremony, or ourselves.

48. Which branch of the United States military was the first to establish the twenty-one gun salute?
    A) The Army
    B) The Navy
    C) The Marine Corps

Every year on the school calendar was the dreaded "Back to School Night" for parents. A brochure was sent to each student's home inviting them to visit the school and talk with their child's teachers. Parents looked at it as being involved in their child's education, and the male teachers looked at it as checking out the students' moms.

Realizing that some parents have an unfavorable perception of school, I was always on guard for outrageous questions or requests to disparage me in front of a group. Usually, this event is mostly attended by those parents who have well-behaved, respectful children, but sometimes, it's an opportunity for some guy to be macho in front of his wife and others. The parents were to follow their child's classroom schedule, and each class was to last ten minutes. The faculty was instructed only to talk about the workings of the school and their philosophy of teaching. Nothing confrontational.

The bell rang and the first group arrived. Although students were told not to accompany their parents, some always did. I welcomed our guests and began my inspirational talk about education and the school. A male parent kept interrupting me with questions to try and minimize my stature as an instructor. “How old are you, Sonny?” I ignored him and continued with my talk about the values of education. “Which one is your desk?” I wanted to say, “The big one, dumb ass,” but I kept my composure and stuck to the agenda. Then I heard, “Does your mommy know you’re out this late?” I paused, silently keeping my emotions intact, and then continued, checking the time for the end of class. “Are you gonna’ ignore me or answer my questions?” Some parents were smiling, and others were embarrassed. By now, I was totally pissed off. My students in attendance were anticipating how I would handle this.

I paused again and looked into the face of the agitator and answered, “Can you be quiet until I finish my presentation?” He angrily replied, “You want to step outside and tell me that?” My career was in jeopardy. I couldn’t show weakness to the parents and students.

Great, I was going to get in a fight with a parent at Back to School Night. The people who came back to school were getting much more than they had expected. The bell rang, and I hoped the altercation was over. Pointing his finger at me, he said, “You’re in big trouble asshole.” I retorted, “Could you please address me as Mr. Asshole when we are at school?” He laughed, stuttered, stammered, and walked away.

I went to the restroom, took a comforting pee, cleared my head, stopped shaking, and went back to the next class like nothing had happened. At that point, I knew I wanted to be a teacher, no matter what the age of the student.

I was teaching a freshman class one day, and, like always, I had the door open. I tried to keep the door open as much as possible to prove to the head dudes on the prowl that we were engaged in some type of instruction at all times. An older gentlemen put his head in the door and knocked on the wall. I acknowledged his presence and asked what he wanted. He said he needed to see his granddaughter, Joy. I asked Joy if the man was her grandfather, and she said yes. I told her to go into the hall and see what he wanted. Joy left the room and began talking to the man, and I resumed teaching the lesson.

The conversation outside became clamorous and unsettling, and I walked toward the door. Before I reached the door, the grandfather had pulled off his belt and was laying some haymakers on Joy’s butt. I called out for him to stop. He continued bashing, and I intervened. The class was at the door enjoying every horrible moment. I stood between Joy and her grandfather. Joy attacked me, shouting, "Leave my grandfather alone." Out from their classrooms came my co-workers, thinking that I had attacked the old man and he was being defended by his granddaughter. My witnesses were the students in my class, and I wasn't sure what they would say.

Security arrived, order was restored, and the interrogation began. Of course, the principal asked, "What just happened?" I turned to my class with a lack of confidence and said, "Ask any of them." Before they could answer, the grandfather and Joy told the true story. I thanked them for their honesty and went back into my classroom. I had to know what my class would have said so I asked them, "What were you going to say if security would have ask you what happened?" The class spokesman responded, "We were doing our work; we didn't see a thing." Then they smiled. I made myself believe that the smile meant they would have told the truth. I think I love those guys.

Every March, state-wide testing took place. It was a standardized test to check the quality of education the school was providing. Security was tight and the rules ridiculous. We had meetings about how to administer the test and how to handle conflicts. The tests were locked away, and before receiving them, teachers had to count the number of tests in front of a test supervisor, who would then recount them to see if teachers were telling the truth. Teachers had to sign how many tests they were taking and place them in a plastic container with the lid closed until reaching the testing site.

The students were not allowed to talk during testing. If they finished before the allotted time, they were to put their heads down on their desk. If a student got sick and soiled the test, the test was to be put in a plastic container and returned with the other tests at the end of the session. We were required to write up any violations and turn them in with the tests. State supervisors walked in and out of the testing sites to make sure the rules were followed. I, unfortunately, remember two violations that happened at my testing site, and I didn't report either of them. To me, they were minor. See if you feel the same way.

I had given all of the security instructions and passed out the tests. The testing group was working quietly. It was possibly the quietest classroom I had ever been in.

I spotted a rather large girl with a low-cut blouse sneaking potato chips out of an open bag in her desk and eating them slowly. She reached into the bag and took out a chip and looked up at me and made eye contact. I shook my head no, indicating for her to stop eating the chips. Caught by surprise, she dropped the chip down into her low-cut blouse lost somewhere between her boobs. She tried to retrieve the chip and it went down further between her breasts. She used one hand to hold one breast back and reached down between them with the other hand, probing her bosom in search of the chip. The other students were not aware of what was taking place.

Trying to diffuse the situation quietly, I walked over to her. She told me the obvious, that she had dropped a chip down her blouse and couldn't find it. Surely she didn't think I was going to help her. Surely you didn't think I was going to help her. I gave her a disgusted look and started to walk away. She again started moving her breasts around looking for the lost chip, and I heard a crack and a crunch. Joyfully, she exclaimed, "I found it!" The class was disturbed, and one student taking the test asked, "What did she find?" No way was I going to say she found a lost potato chip between her boobs. Cleverly, I said, "She is excited because she found the correct answer to her question." Another curious test taker asked, "What was that cracking sound?" I informed, "The question was if a tree falls in the forest and no one sees it, does it make a sound? Now you know the answer is yes."

In another test-taking incident, I tried to save the honor of a young girl. Again, the room was quiet and the students were doing an excellent job of following instructions. Things were so calm I was getting a little sleepy. The room was deadly silent when a girl in the center of the room muffled a little girl sneeze followed by a thunderous blast from her butt. A shot heard around the room, an 8 on the Richter scale. Embarrassed, she quickly put her head down on her desk and covered it with her arms. Trying to come to the rescue, I rejoiced, "I played that same tune this morning in the shower, only louder." I added,

"Men are proud of the experience, aren't we, men?" On cue, some young man sacrificed his honor to reduce the humility of the little girl. Ladies need not worry when a real man is around.

Some schools have been caught changing answers on standardized tests to improve their overall rating. In April of 2013, it was revealed that some Atlanta, Georgia students' test scores showed significant and unexplained increases over the past five years. Educators' salaries rose with rising student test scores. A Fulton County grand jury indicted thirty-five educators, including the former superintendent, in a cheating conspiracy that reached fifty-eight schools.

School administrators have become so obsessed with standardized test scores that a major portion of a school's plan is to teach toward the test, possibly forgoing instruction in many other relevant areas. A school's, and the administration's, reputation are on the line, and some may use illegal means to show improvement.

I sat through many meetings in my school district and read reports about how some area schools outperformed others. Those schools were praised, the administrators were praised, and those teachers were called "master" teachers. The reports never mentioned that the high performing schools were located in the higher socio-economic areas, and the parents have been involved in their child's education since birth. If you want your children to become good students, begin educating them early and establish in them a will to learn and be successful. Can this be accomplished in poor neighborhoods with broken homes and missing parents? I don't know. However, ordaining schools with higher test scores and relating it to better faculties and administrations may not be accurate. A child's education is as important as the clothes they wear, the vehicle they drive, and the food they eat. Assist public schools by being a part of the educational process early and often.

49. What legislation proposed by George W. Bush was to aid public schools in improving education?
A) No Child Left Behind Act
B) Elementary and Secondary Education Act
C) National Child Protection Act

Chapter 29
Teaching Driver's Education

Driving statistics for teen drivers are frightening. In 2013, automobile accidents were the leading cause of deaths among those thirteen to nineteen years old. Sixteen year-olds have the highest crash rate among any age group. The death rate increases among teen drivers with each additional passenger. Fifty-five percent of motor vehicle deaths among teens occur on Fridays, Saturdays, or Sundays. Thirty-seven percent of male drivers involved in fatal accidents were speeding at the time. During my education career, I can recall eight student deaths attributed to automobile accidents at schools where I worked. Cell phones, texting, and music devices have added to the accident-causing distractions.

Besides being a teacher and coach, I was a certified driver's education instructor. The requirements for each student were thirty hours of classroom instruction and six hours of driving instruction. Most of the students were first-time drivers and eager to impress their friends but not necessarily their instructor. Their excitement to drive overcame any fear.

The city and state police would come to class and display gory photos of accidents and show a film in which the victims of an accident were screaming for help. The intent was to show the danger of driving, but some students viewed it as a horror film as if it were not real. They really had no idea!

Teaching in the classroom was safe, but instructing in a moving vehicle had many tense moments. One young lady in class scored perfect on every exam, including the sign test, the state driving exam, and the final exam. I felt good as we got in the vehicle that afternoon. I watched as she was doing everything right, adjusted the seat first, adjusted the mirrors, and looked at the controls. The girl was a rare natural. She was ready to begin, and I was relaxing in the passenger's seat. Looking down at the floorboard, however, she asked, "Now, which one is the brake?" My confidence was shattered.

I was once driving with a self-confident boy who was actually doing well. I always tried to carry on a casual conversation and not appear anxious. I complimented him on his driving and said, "You look like you have some experience driving." He replied, "I drive all the time, Coach." This was going to be an easy day, I thought, until I asked, "Where do you do all your driving?" Without hesitation, he said, "On my Nintendo. This is the first time I've driven in a real car." I countered, "Pull over to the right and stop before my heart does."

Another boy was driving on a short section of the interstate highway. Instead of watching the traffic and the road, he kept looking at the speedometer. He was over the speed limit by a lot when he rejoiced, "Look how fast I'm going!" I rudely interrupted, "Look how fast I'm sweating. Now pick your damn foot up off the accelerator!"

I normally parked the driver's education vehicle in an area beside the football locker room. The student that was driving that particular day would meet me there after school because that's where I finished my day.

As scheduled, a female student was waiting by the car after school. She got behind the steering wheel, and we went over how to back out of a driveway. I instructed her to put her left hand at 12 o'clock on the wheel, place her right arm across the seat, and back up slowly while looking over her right shoulder. I guess I didn't emphasize BACK UP SLOWLY well enough. She floored the accelerator, and we peeled out, jumping the curb behind us. By the time I had wrestled her arms away from the wheel and her legs away from the gas pedal, we were on the fifty-yard line of the practice field in a compromising position. I got up off her and made my way back to the passenger seat. The dust was beginning to settle, and I breathe a sigh of relief. I looked over at her, and she said, "Oops."

One girl was having a trying time keeping the vehicle on the road in a curve. We drove to a rural area with little traffic because there were always three hands on the wheel, her two hands and my left hand from the passenger side. She became more and more frustrated and worse and worse at controlling the car. Finally, she said, "It's not my fault! Why don't they just make all of the roads straight so you don't have to steer?"

I felt like she had a good point.

I walked up on a pretty little girl standing by the vehicle smoking a cigarette. I recognized her from class and checked my calendar. Sure enough, she was my driver for that day. I said, "Marcia Brady, there is no smoking on schools grounds." She said she was nervous about driving. So was I. I told her I wouldn't report her tobacco violation because I understood her apprehension, and the driving lesson was going to be all right. I told the truth about not reporting the tobacco violation and the apprehension, but I lied about the driving lesson being all right.

The girl was Evel Knievel with no sense of direction. Not only was she nervous about her driving, every driver on the street was nervous about her driving. Horns were blowing, fists were raised in defiance, and the middle finger was out en masse. Regretfully, I advised her that for our safety we needed to get off the street. Her solution came quickly, "If you let me smoke while I drive, I'll do better. Smoking calms me down." I saw every person in every car nervously light up a cigarette while she was driving, and no one was calmed down. Sadly, I told her no, but I did consider it.

In my field of education, it was depressing to watch young, wholesome boys and healthy young girls begin the smoking habit. Teens were taught about peer pressure, the health hazards, and the mortality rates of smoking in health class, but it didn't matter. A cigarette was the invitation to a social group or more self-esteem. I had low self-esteem, but in my convoluted world, smoking would lower it even more.

I was around many smokers growing up, and it was socially acceptable at the time. Hollywood portrayed smoking as sensual, sophisticated, and glamorous. Stars and starlets were always featured with a cigarette. Camel brand cigarettes once had an advertisement that stated, "More doctors smoke Camels than any other brand." I have never smoked any tobacco or other product, nor taken a drug illegally in my life. Being drug free means it is good to know my memories are real. That's just the way I think now because of the threats from my mother. I was aware of some classmates, teachers, and coaches that were smokers. Though we are all in a race with Father Time, and he will eventually win, let's be in the race for as long as possible.

Once at school, one of my assistant coaches and I were patrolling the area and restrooms for smokers. In the back area of the school, we smelled cigarette smoke coming from a classroom. That section of the school was at lunch, so no one should have been in the room. We tried to look into the window but the blinds were drawn so we couldn't see. With a master key in hand, we crept to the door, opened it quickly, and said, "Gotcha! Come with us." Imagine our surprise when the culprit was the teacher who remained behind at lunch to smoke her cigarette. The school building was a no-smoking facility. The extent smokers go to is astounding.

At NLU was the sexiest smoker I have ever seen. If everyone could look like her with a cigarette, I would recommend smoking for all. She was a small beautiful girl, straight blonde hair, short tight miniskirt, heavenly body, and a dazzling face and smile. She didn't just hold a cigarette, she held the attention of everyone watching. Where there was smoke, there was desire. I wanted to breathe her second hand smoke. I wanted to take her butt home. She was the Greek goddess of sexy smoking---Cigaritee.

Jest aside, smoking has been responsible for countless tragedies in the United States, but it is such a part of American culture and the economy. We'll just have to hold our breath and live with it.

One of my most respectful and polite drivers was an Iranian boy. He would never come to a complete stop at a stop sign if there was no other traffic. I told him repeatedly that he must stop completely at a stop sign, check for traffic, and then proceed. Then I finished with, "Show those stop signs some respect." He must have translated it as a religious edict because every stop sign we approached after that, he would stop take his hands off the steering wheel place them together as in prayer, and would bow forward letting his forehead touch the steering wheel mumbling, "Stop sign, stop sign." I hope he doesn't do that today; and if he does, I hope he doesn't remember who his driving teacher was.

One time, sympathy got the best of me. I just couldn't tell a sweet little girl how bad she was as a driver. She couldn't make a turn, left or right. I was trying to find an easy turn to give her some confidence and have a reason to compliment her driving. There was a wide street on the left with plenty of margin for error, or so I thought. I told her to turn left onto the next residential street. The family dog was sitting under a tree in the middle of a yard. Again, she started her turn too late. We jumped the curb and crossed the front yard narrowly avoiding the tree. The dog disappeared from sight. Frantically, she cried, "I didn't run over that dog, did I?" I tried to comfort her and said, "Look on the bright side. We didn't hit the tree." I checked for an irate homeowner, and I saw the dog scratching feverishly at the front door trying to get in the house.

On a beautiful spring day, I took my driver on the scenic route around the lake. We had a considerable amount of rain in the days prior, so the water from the lake was near the road. The roadway around the lake had many curves. I told my driver to slow down because he was approaching a curve near the lake. In a panic, he accelerated more, and with my left hand I guided the steering wheel and pushed it to the left, just avoiding the lake. He said, "Thanks, Coach that was embarrassing." I said, "It would be more embarrassing if you had to go to school and tell your friends you hit the lake and ran over a fish."

I was finishing driving with a very good driver. We had some time left so my suggestion was we drive some place where she would be going often. To prepare her, I said, "Where would you like to go?" Her answer came quickly, "The McDonald's drive thru." Away we went to the drive thru. From the speaker I heard, "Welcome to McDonald's. May I take you order?" Without a trace of scruples, she answered, "Nothing, we're just practicing driving through."

I was teaching a summer driver's education class along with three other instructors. Many students take the class in the summer for convenience. The class had an enrollment of 103. While one of the instructors was teaching, the others would walk about the room maintaining order and discipline.

A young student in the back was not paying attention and was talking incessantly to his friend. I wanted to make an example of the young deviant to the rest of the class. I asked the instructor to stop teaching a moment. The remaining 102 students looked back at me. I ordered the misbehaving student to stand up. I lectured him on responsibility, behavior, and respect. Everyone listened, so I felt good. Then, to finish the informative interruption, I told the class I was going to take him outside, call his parents, and possibly remove him from the class.

I saw some of them holding back laughter. I ask the student in a harsh tone, "What's your name?" He said, "Mike Singleton, Jr." The name sounded familiar, but I couldn't place it at that moment. I walked him to the front of the class and grabbed a phone. Still showing off to the class, I told him roughly, "Give me a phone number. "He said, "I have my dad's work number. "I inquired, "Where does the dad of this cheap imitation of a student work?" He numbed me with his response: "He works for the school system. He's the superintendent." Now I remembered the name, Mike Singleton, Parish Superintendent of Schools. Out of 103 students to discipline, I had picked the superintendent's son. Trying to recover, I said, "When you get home, you tell him you almost got kicked out of class....and I think he's doing a great job." The only time the odds are in my favor is when it's lightning.

Chapter 30
Coaching Highs and Lows

If it wasn't for football, my life would have been different. What is the allure of the game? Football attracts by skill, strength, power, athleticism, sanctioned violence, cheer for the home team, your school, colorful uniforms, helmets, bands, cheerleaders, partying, dance lines, heated debates, crowds, bragging rights, publicity, maybe your picture in the newspaper, socializing, a chance at the pretty girls, a better way of life, a career, and being successful. Many people are ignorant of what's happening in the world, but they know everything about their team. In the South, boosters provide money and any other assistance they can to help their team win football games, legally or otherwise. Even in high school football, the teams with the most public support always have the best coaches, the best facilities, the best equipment, and most of all, the best players and the most wins.

50. What teams played in the first intercollegiate football game in the United States?
    A) Harvard and Yale
    B) Rutgers and Princeton
    C) Army and Navy

I worked many happy years as an assistant coach and defensive coordinator at a school with some good athletes. By rule, schools only had the players that lived in their attendance zone. Along came the private schools with players not only in their attendance zone but also anyone else that wanted to attend their school. Therefore, their attendance zone was from coast to coast. They had players from everywhere in the city, some from nearby cities, and occasionally from another state. They were backed by powerful churches, offered a Christian education, and had a network of farm teams, summer camps, and means to attract the best athletes. Public schools could only provide uncertainty. This dilemma remains a controversial topic today. The private schools like it the way it is; the public schools want to change it.

I applied for the vacant head coaching position at a local public school, HHS. I had applied for a head coaching position two other times at more prestigious schools but was passed over for more well-known applicants. Some schools can be selective with whom they hire; some have to take the lesser of the coaching fraternity. That was HHS. Through many prayers and a shortage of good resumes, I got the job.

When I reported for the new job, I immediately became discouraged. All of the confidence I had in the interview process had now become unclear. The school was about 90 percent African-American and so was the team. I didn't know if race was going to be a factor with the team, the school, or the community. My dilemma was how to deal with it. The answer was easy. I was not coaching race; I was coaching football. My defensive teams at the previous school had been mostly African-American, and it didn't matter to me or them. I was simply dedicated to doing the best job for our players.

There are too many clichés in sports. You can have a different one for every day of practice, but clichés don't win games. One statement I read about coaching really defined my belief. You've got to hate losing more than you enjoy winning. That is what drives a coach to work long hours during the week and on weekends to prepare, to strategize, to practice, and to worry. I tried to be a coach that included everyone on the team in our games. Sometimes, it was a rewarding idea, and sometimes, I must have been thinking like a cretin. It's hard to succeed being a warm and fuzzy coach.

Every team has a few players with absolutely no ability, but they still have parents. I felt sorry for two young nerds on one of my teams. Lesson one: coaches should not feel sorry for their players. These two boys were at every practice and went through all the drills. Nevertheless, I was afraid that they would get hurt in a game or scrimmage, so I assigned them jobs like counting plays, keeping statistics, and ranking the cheerleaders of the other team. I was going to reward them with a job well done, and I was going be an all-inclusive coach, so I told them I would let them walk out as captains for the coin toss at the beginning of a game.

They were eager and nervous. I prepped them on what was going to take place. I told them the officials were going to introduce them to the captains of the other team and then they would shake their hands. The official would then advise the visiting team that he was going to flip a coin in the air, and one of the captains of the visiting team would call it. Simple enough.

We were the visiting team. The officials called for our captains, and the two nerds were shaking. Being the coach, I told them if we win the coin toss, we wanted to receive. If not, we would defend the south goal. I pointed out the south goal so there would be no questions. I ended my instructions with an emphatic, "Now go win that coin toss for us!" They were part of the team, and the coin toss was important to us.

I watched from the sidelines as my two beloved nerds served our team as captains. I was feeling good about my decision. I saw the handshakes, and the official was ready for the coin flip. The referee flipped the coin, and it hit the ground. He turned to my captain, and then everyone at midfield started to laugh. He then motioned that the home team would receive. The referee came to the sideline still laughing. I asked him what had happened. He said, "I flipped the coin and told your captain to call it, and he said, 'It's a Kennedy half dollar.' They lost the toss; I had to award the option to the home team."

Had they never been involved in a coin flip? Did I forget to instruct them that on a coin flip you call "heads" or "tails"? Whose idea had it been to send these two nonathletic nerds out there? I became a rabid, demented coach waiting for my victims to return to the sideline. I went to the nerds, and as I approached, one said, "We did our best, Coach." I instantly calmed down. That's all I could ask from a team member. I responded, "Good job, men." I walked quickly away before they could ask, "Can we do it again?"

Not learning my lesson, I tried to be the benevolent coach again. Benevolence is for real life; however, this was football. We had a player that everyone liked but who had no business on a football team. He didn't know anything about football, but he could follow directions. We all protected him the entire season. I made the same promise or mistake with him. I kept telling him he would be the captain one night. We were playing a team that I felt was much less talented, so we should win.

This was the right game to make him the captain. I even factored in that we were the home team, and the opposition would make the call. What could go wrong? Keep reading. I knew that if our opponent's won the coin toss, they would receive. I was going to watch the coin toss from the sideline and indicate to him what to say. I demonstrated, "If I put both arms out that means receive. If I kick with my foot that means kick." I furthered demonstrated on the sideline, and he got it right every time. Arms out receive, foot, kick.

Dripping with sweat, confidence and pride, off he walked to midfield with the official. I was watching closely, confident that nothing could go wrong. The coin was tossed into the air. The visiting team won the toss and elected to receive. I saw my captain look my way just as I instructed. I turned my back to the north end zone and simulated a kick toward the south. As I was simulating my kicking instructions from the sideline, a player walked in front of me, and my soft, simulated kick motion hit him in the butt.

My eyes were still concentrating on my captain at midfield. Then without a warning the official threw a yellow flag, indicating a penalty against us. He walked the ball back fifteen yards to our twenty-five yard line. The referee came to the sideline to explain. "Coach," he said, "I had to call an unsportsmanlike conduct penalty on your captain." Of course, I wanted to know why. The official reported, "When I asked him where he wanted to kick, he said, "I want to kick 'em in the ass." Then the official really pissed me off when he said, "Coach, you really need to get control of your team." Might as well get another penalty, "Hey ref, he meant kick you in the ass." Fifteen yards, unsportsmanlike conduct on the coach. We started the game kicking off from our ten-yard line but the crowd was on our side all night. We won big by the score of 42-0.

Still working on my Coach of the Year credentials, I had to endure yet another terrible player. He kept asking me when he was going to play. Finally, in a game we were comfortably ahead, I called for him. We had just scored a touchdown and were preparing to kickoff. As they say in the coaching profession, "I coached him up." I told him to line up at the end of the kick off alignment next to me.

He was in position eleven next to our sideline so I could coach him during the play. It was a bad decision. The referee blew his whistle, indicating to kick the ball. Our place kicker approached the ball, and I was instructing, “Wait, wait, wait.” As the ball was kicked into the air, I yelled, “Now go tackle the player with the ball.” He did just as I said. The player was down, the whistle had blown and the player was walking off the field. Running from across the field was my prodigy, and he tackled the unsuspecting opposing player just before he reached his team’s side line. The official looked at me with scorn and said, “What the hell was that?” All I could think of was, “You’re damn right I ordered a code red!”

A lot of administrators are former coaches. When they attend games, they are free of emotions and like to give foolish advice to enhance their head-dude “I know more than you do about everything” personality. One night we were in a close nothing to nothing game, and it was almost half time. We ran an end sweep, and our running back fumbled the ball. Overcome with negative emotions, I shouted at no one in particular, “Son of a bitch!” It was loud enough for our principal to hear. He walked up to me on the sidelines with his expressionless face and elite attitude and said, “Coach, you need to be more positive with your players.” Loathingly, I looked at him and said, “The son of a bitch made a good run before he fumbled the ball. Is that positive enough?”

In high school, our football seasons began with a jamboree. As many as four teams were involved, and teams would play one quarter against each other team. The problem was always the uniforms. Since so many teams were involved at one location, sometimes the jersey colors would be similar. We were wearing orange jerseys and orange helmets in one quarter, and our opposition had maroon jerseys and maroon helmets. Both team's wore white pants. It was confusing, and the official admitted to me after a penalty that he wasn’t sure which team committed the foul. He said he couldn’t tell the teams apart. I told him it was easy to tell us apart. Our players were wearing the white pants with the yellow stains in the front and the brown stains in the back.

On our schedule was a perennial, powerful, parochial school. I didn’t like when teams brought religion into a football game. Does God really care who wins? Is one team trying to make the other team look even more unworthy? In one of our losses to the Christian school, one of their players had a sign that read, "Jesus got our back." I feel that way, also, but not in a football game. One of our players saw the sign and turned to me, "Coach, does Jesus really have their back?" I told him, "It's not true." The player said, "How do you know?" I told him, "I looked all over the stands and I didn't see Jesus anywhere."

Their coaches and administrators were always very cordial and extended the best they had to offer to us. They presented an atmosphere of family and Christian values and then would go out and ridiculously beat us severely. We never beat them, but we made them nervous a few times.

After one of the losses, their coach-preacher asked me if I would like to join them in the center of the field to pray and communicate with God and be thankful for our blessings. I said, "You mean like the blessing we just received tonight? I've already communicated with God and he told me to get our asses on the bus and get the hell out of here."

Nevertheless, the coaching profession is filled with the greatest of guys. They are made up of a lot of man, sprinkled with little boy enthusiasm, and have a penchant for not telling the truth about their team. The camaraderie is infectious, but on game nights, you don't give them the respect given to a bad mother-in-law. After the game, you can talk and laugh with them into the night because they are like family.

The coach I admired growing up was Tom Landry, the first coach of the Dallas Cowboys. He was quiet, religious, innovative, and unfazed by the popularity of being the head coach of "America's Team." So different than most coaches, he taught Sunday school classes on the mornings before home games. He was married fifty-one years to his wife, Alicia, until his death in 2000.

He joined the United States Army Air Corps during World War II after his brother was shot down and killed while flying a B-17 across the North Atlantic. He completed thirty combat missions and survived a crash landing. His biography is one of my favorite books. He held a Master's Degree in Industrial Engineering. Not your typical ex-jock coach. He played in the NFL for the New York Giants, making the All-

Pro team and also served as a player-assistant coach, which is unheard of. His Dallas teams won two Super Bowls, five NFL titles, and thirteen divisional titles, and his twenty-career playoff victories are the most of any coach in the NFL. As head coach of the Cowboys, his teams had twenty consecutive winning seasons. He was inducted into the NFL Hall of Fame in 1990.

What makes a good coach? Why are some successful and others fail on the big stage? Coach Bum Phillips of the Houston Oilers once answered that question in a unique way when referring to Don Shula, coach of the Miami Dolphins. With his Texas drawl, he said Shula could "Take his'n and beat your'n, or he could take your'n and beat his'n."

Even as a high school coach, you are judged by wins and losses and the many witnesses sitting in the stands on Friday nights. Your success or failure is there for everyone to see. You are shouted at from the stands and approached by angry parents after some games. Sometimes, you are called into the principal's office on Monday mornings to explain your team's play and your behavior or remarks to others. After a loss, my wife always asked the same question when I arrived home, "Why did you lose?" My standard answer was, "Little One, we didn't score enough points." After a loss, your wife is ugly, you can't sleep, you can't eat, you don't want to see anyone, and if you do, they had better not ask you about the game.

On the other hand, many unexpected things happen to remind you how fortunate you are to be in this profession. I swell with emotion when I see a former player, and he begins with "Hey, Coach, remember the time...." The title "Coach" is not like president, governor, or senator; it's better! Even when your time is over, you are still, and always will be, "Coach." You will forever live in their yearbooks and memories as part of the best times of their lives. All coaches want their players to be successful on the field, in school, and for the rest of their lives.

I had a great player once, but he was an under achiever in the classroom. His math teacher told me he needed help, so I volunteered to help him during our athletic hour. He gave me his math assignment, and I thought back to my teaching methods class in college. I recalled, "If possible put the lesson in terms the student is familiar with." The first problem was if A > B, and B is > C then ____ is the greatest. I thought I would put the problem in football perspective so he would better understand. My presentation was "If this was a football team and player A is better than player B, and player B is better than player C, who would be the best player on the team?" He said, "Aw, come on, Coach, that's easy." I saw the light bulb turn on in his head. I said, "Then what's the answer?" He said, "Me, Coach, you know I'm the best player on the team." Tutorial lesson number one was over. I verified the fact that he was an underachiever and methods class in college was useless.

The moral of this next account is "Don't always trust your players." This story is rated **R** for nudity. Once again, I had let my emotions get involved in a football decision.

We had a talented, but troubled, running back on our team. He was a great player as a sophomore, ineligible as a junior, and struggling in many phases of life as a senior. After his sophomore season, he had received interest from some SEC schools, such as Tennessee and LSU. I wanted him to have a good senior year. He was a natural athlete that could play many positions and succeed at all of them.

The first hour of the day was my head coaching period when I usually took care of football business, such as phone calls or meeting with scouts, players, parents, or the principal. The second hour of the school day, I was in the classroom teaching.

Dale knocked at my classroom door and said he had left some homework in the locker room and wanted to go finish it. The school manual strictly prohibited any teacher from giving school keys to students. So what did I do? I gave my athletic keys to Dale so he could finish his homework in the locker room. I wanted him to keep his grades current and remain eligible. Who would know?

After a considerable length of time, Dale had not returned, and doubt about his homework progress entered my mind. Near the end of the hour, an office worker came to my classroom and said the principal needed to see me. I knew this wasn't going to be good, and I knew Dale had something to do with it. I walked toward the school office, and the secretary said, "Go right in. He's waiting for you." I was not prepared for a defense because I didn't know the charges. I would admit to giving my keys to Dale and say I didn't know anything else.

The principal opened with, "Did you give your athletic keys to Dale?"

"Yes, I did," I said. He already had me for breaking the rules.

He continued, "Do you know that's against school policy?"

I confessed that I did. I surmised that Dale had gotten caught with my set of keys. The next question was predictable. "Why did you give Dale your keys?"

I said, "Dale needed to do his homework. I was trying to teach him to be responsible." Then it got complex.

The principal said, "The custodian caught Dale and a young lady in the training room. Dale was getting undressed. What should I do to you, Dale, and the young lady?"

We were all caught with our pants down. All I could say was, "You're the boss."

He called for Dale to come to the office. I was trying to save all of us, so I ripped into Dale. "Dale, you let the team down, you let the young lady down, you let your parents down, and you let me down. Was it worth it?" I was as convincing as Atticus Finch in *To Kill a Mockingbird.*

Dale hung his head. I felt sorry for him, and so did the principal. Then Dale looked up and said, "Yea, Coach, she was worth it." No one felt sorry for Dale anymore. I was reprimanded in my personnel folder, Dale was suspended for the rest of the week, the young lady was exonerated, and we lost the game. I got Dale to tell the truth even though I didn't want to. What a lousy coach.

However, many others joined in for the delightful, heartwarming times at HHS. The faculty and custodial staff proudly wore tee shirts supporting our team. One young custodian really got carried away. He had been out of high school for only a year or two. Other than his custodial shirt with his name on it, you couldn't distinguish him from the other students at school.

He came to my office one day when no one was there. He said, "Hey, Coach, let me play in the game tonight. They won't know who I am." I told him all the reasons why he could not: it's against the rules, you're not a student, you're too old, the principal will find out, and I will get fired. Then he came back with, "I talked to the custodian at the other school, and he said he was going to play." I finally convinced him that no way it was going to happen. I told him to get back to doing his usual lousy job of cleaning up the school.

We had a good football player who rarely came to school. When we began to win some games, his attendance was much better. One morning the phone rang in my office. It was his mother, and she was frantic. She said she had looked all over the house and the neighborhood and couldn't find Michael. I told her I would check it out and call her back. I looked at Michael's schedule and went to his first hour class, and there he was. I called his mother back and informed her he was safe and in school. She said, "Next time, he better tell me if he's goin' to school." Athletics makes people do strange things.

Once we were traveling to a town across the river to play a very good team. Their record was 5-0 and they had a very good coach and a lot of success. Our record was 2-3, but we were playing well. We had a good night and upset them 26-7. We boarded the bus for the return trip home. The district's school busses are equipped with radios so the bus drivers can communicate with each other. We were sitting on the bus, quietly glowing in our unforeseen success. My seat was always behind the bus driver. Another bus driver called and asked, "How did HHS do tonight?" Happily, our driver shouted, "We won 26-7!" The driver on the radio said, "Girl, do you know what I asked you? I don't want to know the score. I want to know if HHS won." Again our driver said, "We won 26-7." Unbelieving, the other driver said, "I don't believe you, I'll just look in the paper tomorrow." I turned around and looked at the players on the bus, and I saw thirty sets of smiling teeth in the dark. No one wanted to believe that we had won. That night we had overcome the odds, I was overcome with emotion at those smiling faces. I was so proud to be part of THEIR success.

HHS had a large special needs department because our school did not have a second floor; therefore, many handicapped students were housed there. The special needs students went to lunch first. Like every other student, they would race to be first in the lunch line. My foot served as a speed bump more than once for speeding wheelchairs. One particular student stopped to talk to me one Friday at lunch. We had played a Thursday night game and won. He was excited about two things and kept repeating them. "Coach, we won last night and I saw it on my own television! Coach, we won last night and I saw it on my own television!" I recall that statement today and still remember the delight in his eyes. The following week I gave him his own HHS football tee shirt. I made the little dude happy. The little dude hugged me and made me happier.

During a game, a coach is thinking constantly. You must come up with an offensive play or a defensive call within twenty-five seconds, so you have to think ahead but keep a perspective on the current happenings on the field. It is not a time to be talking to a coach unnecessarily, especially if you don't have anything good to say.

Again, we were playing the parochial school power, and again they we were winning. Since we were playing at their school, they provided security for the game. Like most teams, they hire people they know, known as "homers." Their team was doing well, and we were struggling against the superior opponent. The police officer working our sideline said to me, "If this continues, I'm gonna' get out the yellow crime tape and put it around the field. This is a crime scene. Y'all are getting' murdered." I'm sure he used that line every week, but he didn't get a laugh from me. I should have had someone tape a gun under the bench. I would have shot him, left the gun, and taken the cannoli, just like in *The Godfather.* I still have a lot of Giovanni in me.

I have observed that the ones that know nothing about football give the most advice. Most parents believe their son is the best player on the team, and the coach doesn't know it. They also believe the coach should let him play and get him a scholarship. One father followed me around at practice and after games, wanting to know why his son didn't get to play. Tactfully, I explained that he was not better than the players ahead of him. I put a little Sweet 'N Low on it (artificially sweetened the conversation). He's still young, he works hard, he is getting better, and his day will come.

After the next game, which we won handily 30-6, he found me

on the field and said, "My son didn't get to play tonight." I had seen enough of this man, who was spoiling my "thrill of victory." I said, "I know. If he had played, we would have lost." I knew I would be in the head dude's office on Monday morning. Sometimes coaching requires a heart and sometimes you must be heartless.

Another annoyance was players wanting to know if college scouts were asking about them. Some players received college letters of interest, and most couldn't get a letter from home. A big offensive lineman fit the old category of "looks like Tarzan but plays like Jane," but he didn't think so. Every week, he would ask, "Coach, have any scouts asked about me?"

While I was passing out the college letters before practice one day, in front of the whole squad I said, "Tarzan, two scouts came by today asking about you." Pleased, and in front of the whole team he said, "What did they say?" Regretfully, I said, "They wanted to know how many boxes of cookies you wanted to buy this year." The players laughed. Not getting the put down, he tried again, "No, Coach, what did they really say?" Again, I tried my best to tell him, "They said you look cute in your uniform." He said, "Did they really?" Now I can say, "Looks like Tarzan, plays like Jane, thinks like Cheetah." (Cheetah was Tarzan's chimp companion).

Hecklers from the stands are really irritating. I tried to ignore them, but sometimes I had to acknowledge that I heard them. My philosophy was we wanted to be a running team with the ability to pass when we wanted to, not when we had to. In today's game, most fans want to see teams pass more and run less. You have to be patient when running the ball because the goal is to make first downs, use time off the clock, and eventually score. On one occasion, I threw a pass because I had to. Here's how it happened.

Some wanna-be coach kept bellowing from the stands, "Throw the ball." Maybe he was trying to impress his wife and those around him. He continued to shout, "Throw the ball, Coach. You've got to throw the ball, Coach. I won't shut up until you throw the ball." I walked over to the ball bag and retrieved an old ball. I saw him in the stands and pointed at him. I threw the ball toward him in the stands. He reacted as if he had two fly swatters for hands. He dropped the pass. I looked at him and said, "That's why we don't throw the ball."

The second time we made the state playoffs at HHS, we were seeded number thirty-one of thirty-two teams. I knew we were better than that, but we had played such a demanding schedule our rating was low because of four losses. Nevertheless, we had to play the number-two seed in the playoffs at their home field. Number thirty-one against number two on the road. The school administration arranged spectator busses for those students who wanted to make the 3 1/2 hour bus trip to the game. Eight busloads of rowdy students signed up, most to get out of school early and to have a traveling party. HHS had not been in the playoffs very often, so the thrill of the game, and the bus ride, was an opportunity to be wild.

During the pre-game warm up, our fans arrived. They were loud, boisterous, and little bit smutty. A state trooper walked up to me on the field and told me I needed to go calm our student section down. He thought they might be a problem. I thought, "He had the uniform, the gun, and a badge, why ask me? It they are too loud, fire a warning shot in the air." I was tired of this hometown intimidation. I walked over to the stands and loudly said, "The officer told me to ask you to calm down, you're scaring the home team." Then, they became very loud, very boisterous, and a lot smuttier. Could I have been arrested for inciting a riot? Our players fed off the crowd and we were primed to play.

The team we were playing had the nickname, The Golden Tornadoes. They had a clever way of entering the field. They would sound a siren, and the PA announcer would say, "Tornado Warning!" and they would run onto the field to the cheers from their stands.

As the game progressed, we were playing at our best. Every time we did something positive, our students would simulate the tornado siren to anger the home team. As the game was in the final minutes, we were ahead 18-8. Our students were on the verge of cascading from the stands and flooding the field. What is the sound for a tsunami warning? We intercepted a pass, clinching the victory. We ran out the clock and the grand celebration began. Everyone was in high spirits, except the eight bus drivers who had to endure 3 1/2 more hours of the celebration on the drive back home.

Two of the most bizarre incidents that happened took place while I was the head coach at HHS. Each year in October we would play our cross-town rival at Independence Stadium during the time of the State Fair. There was always a big crowd because of the rivalry, and the game ticket allowed you on the fair grounds. After the game, most of the fans would go to the fair and enjoy the rides, food, side shows, and would brag about winning the game.

We won the game 12-6 and were preparing to leave the field to get on the bus for the ride back to school. In the north end zone near the closest entrance to the State Fair, I saw two of our players take of their helmets and shoulder pads, place them on the field, and bolt out of the stadium to the fair. They were dressed in their navy blue game pants and their white jerseys with navy blue numbers. They were easy to spot among fair goers.

As the rest of team returned to the bus, I told the principal that two of our players had departed and had gone to the fair in uniform. He quoted the parish rule that if a player rode the bus to the game, he must ride the bus home. He held up the two team buses and sent me to the fair to locate the two runaways. I jogged from the parking lot to the gate entrance and began my search. It was Friday night around ten o'clock, and the grounds were crowded. I saw many of our students at the fair and asked if they had seen the two players. No one had seen them. I asked police officers, strangers, ride operators, and game hosts. No sight of two fairgoers in blue and white football uniforms.

I went back to the bus. The parking lot near the stadium was almost vacant, but the team busses remained. I told the principal that I couldn't find them. What was a funny situation was now annoying. I was more irritated at the principal than I was at the two runaways.

I wanted the busses to return the rest of the team to school, and he and I could look for the two escapees and take them home in his car. He kept insisting that they must ride the bus back to school. Again, he quoted me the parish rule and sent me back to the fair. I borrowed ten dollars from him as I again went to the fair. This time my plan had changed. I bought a corn dog, fresh lemonade, and sat down and watched the crowd, hoping the two players would pass by. I thought back to my high school days at the fair. After more time had passed, I saw a cheap toy plastic fish on the ground, a prize so trivial it was thrown away. I picked it up and headed back to the still waiting busses.

By this time, my motor was running hotter than the busses. I walked up the principal, quoted him the parish rule, told him where the "good" corn dog stand was, advised him to be careful on the rides, gave him the plastic fish, and finished with, "Enjoy your night at the fair." I got on the bus and told the bus driver to take us back to school. The team cheered, and the last I saw of the principal that night was when he was walking toward the fair still carrying the plastic fish. I hope he took my advice about the corn dog stand and the rides. I didn't want him to miss our Monday morning meeting.

The other bizarre incident happened at school before we had departed for a game. The team was dressed and quietly lounging in the locker room. The coaching staff was going over the game plan when two police officers entered. They gave me a name and asked if he was in the locker room. I pointed him out, and they walked to him and handcuffed him. He was one of our best players. As he was escorted in his football uniform out of the locker room, he said, "Coach, take my helmet and shoulder pads to the game. If I get out, I still want to play." I watched as they placed him in the police vehicle. One of the officers came back to inform me that he had been breaking into cars in the parking lot.

Later on, we left for the game. During the game, I heard a familiar voice calling me from the stands. There he was, still in his uniform, eating a box of popcorn, "Coach, did you bring my helmet and shoulder pads? Put me in. I want to play." With the score as it was, we could have used him. I said, "Finish your popcorn and check with me later." I never heard from him again.

Coaching at a needy school had its own unique situations. The players were dedicated and worked hard, but there were circumstances we had to work around. School was out at 3:30 P.M., and our practices would start around 3:45. Some of the players had jobs, so often I heard, "Coach, I have to be at work at five." "Coach, I can't practice today. My momma has to work late, and I have to baby sit." "Coach, I have remedial classes at 5 o'clock on Monday and Wednesday so I can graduate." At times, this one was requested, "Coach, I can't practice today. I have to meet with my parole officer." We can't look at life through our own prescription glasses. We can't see just what we want to see. We can't be blurred to the needs of others. Sometimes, you have to have a conversation with yourself, possibly make a sacrifice, and do something good for the needy.

The Hatfields and the McCoys, the Montagues and the Capulets, Coke verses Pepsi, the haves against the have-nots. If you are a have not, you can't go back in time and get the respect you thought you deserved or that girl that passed on you for a better life style. Many have escaped have-not status through education, sports, entertainment, talent, and good looks, but even these have only escaped the economic and social phases of have not status. They seldom escape the emotional phase.

If you are a have-not, you can get an education and hope for the best. You can learn a skill and hope for the best. If not, you can have a good work ethic, and "get after it." I like the haves and the have-nots. The few haves I know always treat me with respect and kindness, and so do the have-nots. It is not criminal to be a have or a have-not. Don't dislike one because you are a member of the other. Maybe our lives will not always be on earth. Maybe there is a place where people don't have to live as haves and have-nots.

My first game as a head coach was a dream come true, but I will not remember it that way. Tragedy found its way into the occasion. HHS was opening the season on a Thursday night. We were the visiting team at a game in a bordering city. Our opponents were very good and very well-coached. They had a lot of success in the past, and it was going to continue. We played a competitive game and lost 28-20. I was satisfied with our team's effort and felt a little sense of accomplishment even though we lost.

We had a tough running back named Robert. He was a little strange, but there was no doubting him as a football player. He had come to HHS from a nearby private school. Like some others, he was not going to play as much there, or he had some problems with the school.

We were glad to have him.

During the first half of the game, he became disoriented and came to the sidelines. The certified trainer from the hospital checked him out and told us to hold him out the rest of the game. Robert took off his uniform and sat on the bench. His dad came down from the stands and talked to the trainer. The trainer advised him to take him to the emergency room and have him checked out. Robert and his dad decided to stay and watched the rest of the game.

After the game, Robert got into his dad's truck, and the two were going to the emergency room for Robert to be checked by medical professionals. While in the truck, Robert stopped breathing. By the time they arrived at the hospital emergency room, Robert was unconscious and had to be put on a ventilator. Although hospital personnel revived him, he had brain damage.

I was unaware of what had taken place. I accompanied the team back to school after the game. After the players had left, the coaches started washing the game uniforms, cleaned up the locker room, and made copies of the game film to be traded the next day.

When I got home around midnight, I received a telephone call telling me of the situation. I called the principal, and we went to the hospital. It was obvious from the first look that the situation was serious. Robert lay in the bed attached to a breathing machine. He was motionless and his eyes were closed. We tried to talk to him but got no response. After a while, Robert made a little improvement. He could sit up in bed and breathe on his own, but he did not recognize anyone or speak. Nurses had to feed him and assist him in all daily routines. He was eventually transferred to a facility in Texas where he would remain. Football has an ugly side.

While I was an assistant coach, another catastrophic injury took place. We had a very good defensive back and receiver that had an injured ankle. We decided to hold Will out of the next game because we felt we could win without him. However, he dressed and went with the team to the game.

We were ahead the entire game, but the opposition started to rally in the third quarter. We sent Will into the game on defense. The opposition threw a pass complete across the middle of the field, and Will made the tackle, breaking two vertebrae in his neck. He was taken off the field by paramedics in an ambulance. He was paralyzed from the neck down.

Years later, Will came to a junior varsity football game. He was married and had become a preacher. I like to believe that we are all equal, but Will is a better man than most.

Football is a dangerous game. This is known by the players, coaches and fans; yet, the love affair with the game continues. For those that consider the dangers too much of a risk, they choose not play. Parents that watch their children play are rooting more for safety than they are for a win.

Coaches and players understand the phrase, "Leave it all on the field," which means you always try your best on every play. You do your job for the success of the team. You give maximum effort until there is no effort left in your body. There is only one response to getting knocked down in football. You get up and accept the challenge of the next play. No matter the score, no matter the opponent, no matter the odds, you sacrifice yourself for the game. Why? My reasons won't convince you, but here they are: Football was a blessing to me and has been to countless others, and will continue to be. You don't play the game for the glory; you play because you love the sport and you are part of a team. I loved training with the team, preparing for games, surviving a tough practice, doing my assignment to make a play successful, relying on others, having others depend on me, the feeling of winning the game, understanding that my ability and opportunity are gifts from God. Football laid the foundations for friendships that will last forever and for moral lessons like not giving in to adversity and to keep trying and trying and trying to accomplish goals for the rest of your life.

There have been many recent studies on football related injuries, and the findings are not good. Therefore, sayings like "he just got his bell rung," it's just a stinger," "walk it off," "play through the pain," and "tough it out" are not used anymore. Concussions are treated with extreme caution.

Concussions are a form of brain injury. Researchers say the constant hitting of the helmet and the movement of the brain inside the skull can cause long-term harm at all levels of play, from youth leagues to the NFL. (I got my brain condition the old fashioned way, through heredity and physical discipline from my Italian father.) Doctors claim that repeated multiple blows to the head may lead to behavioral changes similar to dementia. They report that conditions may range from neurological disease to depression-related suicidal thoughts. The condition is called CTE, Chronic Traumatic Encephalopathy. In addition to CTE are the numerous injuries to knees, shoulders, arms, backs, hands, permanently disabling injuries, as well as heat-related deaths.

Four thousand former NFL football players have joined in lawsuits against the league for concealing information about the harm caused by concussions.

Popular player, Junior Seau took his own life in 2012 at age forty-three. He had completed a twenty-year NFL career in 2010. Studies by the National Institute of Health concluded that Seau suffered from Chronic Traumatic Encephalopathy.

Dave Duerson, a nineteen-year veteran of the NFL, died from a self-inflicted gunshot to the chest in 2011 at age fifty. He left a text message to his family saying he wanted his brain to be used for research at the Boston University School of Medicine. Neurologists at Boston University confirmed that he suffered from a neurodegenerative disease linked to concussions.

An autopsy on Ray Easterling, another former NFL suicide victim, also determined that CTE was the underlying major condition that accounted for his emotional difficulties.

Other tragic stories are the lives of NFL veterans Mike Webster, John Mackey, and Jim McMahon.

Lawyers are closing in. Will lawsuits become so overwhelming that high school football and possibly some colleges won't be able to afford the cost of subsidizing the game? Will rule changes alter the game into an imitation of what it once was? I have read about the medical difficulties of some former players. Most seem to have survived their careers without impact-related difficulties. Is it modern medicine, a change in culture, or an attack on the game of football? Is football on the endangered species list?

Part Six

Answers 47-50

47. How many amendments make up the Bill of Rights?
    B) Ten
    The Bill of Rights is the collective name for the first ten amendments to the Constitution. They guarantee a number of personal freedoms for citizens of the United States. They were introduced to Congress by James Madison and became law on December 15, 1791. There have been twenty-seven amendments to the United States Constitution of 1787

48. Which branch of the military was the first to establish the twenty-one gun salute?
    B) The Navy
    The custom stems from naval tradition, where a warship would fire its cannon harmlessly out to sea until all ammunition was spent to show that it was disarmed, signifying the lack of hostile intent.

49. What legislation proposed by George W. Bush was to aid public schools in improving education?
    A) No Child Left Behind Act
    The law requires all public schools receiving federal funds to administer a state-wide standardized test annually to all students.

50. What teams played in the first intercollegiate football game in the United States?
    B) Rutgers and Princeton
    The game was played on November 6, 1869 at 3 P.M. on a plot of turf at Rutgers University in New Brunswick, New Jersey. The game was played with rugby like rules. The Rutgers' players donned scarlet scarves around their heads to identify with their school.

Conclusion

My writing venture has come to an end. I apologize to William Shakespeare for not using *thee, thou* or *whence* anywhere in the book. I tried. The light from the end of the long tunnel of the past is beginning to dim. The time machine has returned to the present, and yesteryear is left behind once again in the pages of high school annuals and the minds of aging friends. It is mystifying how fast time can pass.

I could not have completed my personal journey without a little help from my friends. During our lifetime we witness things that we didn't know could exist. We accomplish things that were once part of our doubts and dreams. A more youthful generation will replace our stories with theirs, and we will return to obscurity.

I went from Giovanni to Johnny and lived during some historic times along the way. What an adventure! I often think of my teammates and friends, Jack, Don, and Mitch. I especially remember them in my prayers on Fridays, game day, which seems like the appropriate day of the week for our spiritual reunion. I pray it will be God's will that one day we will delightfully be reunited again for some more joy and laughter. Lastly, being the incredibly special person you are, I ask for your acceptance.

Johnny-Giovanni Piazza

Jack Don Mitch & Me

www.ingramcontent.com/pod-product-compliance
Lightning Source LLC
Chambersburg PA
CBHW060235050426
42448CB00009B/1450
9780692594957